good food
for friends

good food

for friends

over 175 recipes and ideas
for easy entertaining

Special photography by Marie-Louise Avery, Jean Cazals and Philip Webb

Published by BBC Worldwide Ltd,
Woodlands, 80 Wood Lane,
London W12 0TT

First published 2001
Copyright © BBC Worldwide 2001
Recipes by the *BBC Good Food Magazine* team: Mary Cadogan, Angela Nilsen,
Vicky Musselman and Kate Moseley.
For a full list of photographers, please see page 144.

ISBN 0 563 53412 5

Edited by Lewis Esson
Commissioning editor: Vivien Bowler
Project editor: Sarah Lavelle
Copy editor: Christine King
Art direction: Lisa Pettibone
Designer: Sarah Jackson

Set in Clarendon and Helvetica
Printed and bound in Italy by LEGO Spa
Colour separations by Kestrel Digital Colour Ltd, Chelmsford, Essex

Contents

Introduction

If *BBC Good Food Magazine* is about anything it is about enjoying food, and the belief that this pleasure should be experienced as much by the cook as by everyone else who shares the meal. The philosophy also extends to the experience of cooking for special occasions and 'having friends over'. It is all too easy to forget that the focus of such a meal is the conviviality of the occasion – the pleasure of being in such a warm and amiable gathering – and that when guests come to your table they come as much for your company as for a demonstration of your culinary prowess.

For this reason, the focus of recipes in the magazine, and in this book, tend towards the concept of 'relaxed entertaining'. Recipes are such that you won't be worn out by multiple reductions of a sauce or be tearing your hair out trying to construct some elaborate assembly minutes before your guests arrive. As much as possible – however impressive the results – the recipes are generally all fairly simple and straightforward to follow.

Where appropriate, the recipes in this book also provide you with details of how you can prepare as much of the dish ahead of time as possible, to help minimize last-minute fuss and clear some time just before the meal for you to spend with your guests. Where necessary, there are even full instructions for freezing and reheating parts – or all – of a dish.

As a further aid to easing your way to a memorable meal, there are also helpful notes on choosing wines and other drinks to complement almost all the dishes in the book. Additionally, at the end, there is a detailed guide to menu planning – with lots of useful and practical hints – and a host of suggested menus for all occasions using the recipes in the book.

Throughout the book, too, you will find handy features on subjects such as garnishing, buying the best and freshest of fish, useful techniques including frying and roasting, and simple but spectacular ways of ringing the changes with basic recipes like mashed potatoes and custard.

Some useful basic recipes

Possibly the easiest and best way to impress with your food is to make sure it has a good strong flavour. Buying the best and freshest ingredients you can find and afford will help – especially if you try to use seasonal produce wherever possible.

Another sure-fire taste-boosting trick is to use your own home-made stock instead of cubes (or you could even try the great new range of fresh stocks now widely available) whenever a stock is at the heart of a dish – as with, say, a soup, a sauce or a risotto. Providing you plan ahead, stock is simplicity itself to make, fairly inexpensive to put together and always tastier than bought – helping to impart a genuinely home-made flavour. Using it is so much more satisfying for the cook.

In the same way, a good marinade will add strong full flavour to the plainest of ingredients, such as chops or chicken portions, when they are to be simply roasted, grilled or barbecued.

Classic chicken stock
To make 1.7 litres/3 pints stock, put 1kg/2lb 4oz chicken or turkey carcass (make up the weight with uncooked drumsticks or wings if necessary) in a large wide pan and just cover with cold water (about 2 litres/3½ pints). Halve a large onion and stud each half with cloves. Add to the pot with 2 chopped carrots, 1 sliced leek, 1 sliced celery stick, 1 tsp black peppercorns and a bouquet garni. Bring to the boil, lower the heat and cook gently, uncovered, for 1–1½ hours. Skim the surface occasionally with a slotted spoon. Strain through a fine sieve set over a bowl (not a colander as the holes are too big).

Vegetable stock
Vegetable stocks are far quicker to make, as well as being lighter and milder than meat stocks. In summer, add fennel and tomatoes, or add wild mushrooms in the autumn. Avoid using cabbage, as it can make stock taste bitter. To make 1.5 litres/2¾ pints stock, put 600g/1lb 5oz mixed chopped vegetables (e.g., carrots, onions, leeks) into a pan with 2 unpeeled garlic cloves, 4 peppercorns and 1 cored, deseeded and roughly chopped red pepper. Add 1.4 litres/2½ pints cold water and a bouquet garni. Bring to the boil, then simmer gently for 35 minutes. Strain through a fine sieve set over a bowl.

Fish stock

Ask the fishmonger or fish counter at your supermarket to set aside about 1kg/2lb 4oz of fish trimmings, fish heads and bones. To make the stock, put these trimmings in a large pan with 1 chopped onion, 1 chopped carrot, 1 chopped leek, 12 black peppercorns and a bouquet garni. Pour in 150ml/¼ pint white wine and enough water to cover. Bring to the boil, then simmer for 30 minutes. Strain through a fine sieve or muslin and season if necessary. Return the stock to a clean pan, bring to the boil and reduce it further to improve the flavour.

Court-bouillon (for poaching fish and shellfish)

If you're poaching a whole fish, you can simply add a few vegetables, herbs and lemon slices to the liquid, but for best results make a court-bouillon first. Stud a large, peeled onion with a few cloves, slice a couple of carrots and a leek and put them in a large pan with a bouquet garni, 2 lemon slices, a tablespoon of white wine vinegar and equal quantities of dry white wine or cider and water – about 700ml/1¼ pints of each. Simmer for 30 minutes, then allow to cool and strain before use. After you've poached fish or shellfish in the court-bouillon, it becomes a good strong stock, so you can use it for a soup or sauce.

Freezing stock

Home-made stock freezes very well. Allow it to cool, then chill overnight to allow the fat to rise to the surface. Skim off the fat with a slotted spoon, then freeze the stock in quantities you are likely to use. Line a freezerproof container with a labelled freezer bag (one stock looks much like another once frozen). Pour the stock into the bag, leaving room for expansion, seal and freeze – once frozen, the bag can be removed from the container. Frozen stock will keep for up to 3 months.

Intensify the flavour

For a more concentrated stock, reduce it by one-third after straining and skimming – allow it to cool and then freeze it in ice-cube trays. The frozen cubes quickly defrost into soups, gravies, sauces and casseroles as they cook and will add richness to sauces.

Dark sticky marinade (For red meat, sausages, chicken, chops and spare ribs)

To make enough for 6 people: mix together 3 tbsp dark muscovado sugar, 6 tbsp tomato ketchup, 2 tbsp orange juice, 1 tbsp Worcestershire sauce, 2 tsp chopped fresh oregano or 1 tsp dried, and 1 tsp English or Dijon mustard. Season well, then use to coat the meat. Leave for at least 30 minutes or overnight to marinate.

Citrus marinade (For fish and chicken)

To make enough for 6 people: mix together 2 finely chopped garlic cloves, 2 finely chopped shallots, the grated zest and juice of ½ lime and ½ lemon (reserve the other halves for serving), 1 tbsp crushed fennel or coriander seeds, 2 tbsp chopped fresh parsley, tarragon, dill, fennel or basil and

6–8 tbsp light olive oil. Season well and use to coat the fish or chicken. Leave to marinate for about 30 minutes.

Mustard and herb marinade (For sausages, pork chops and vegetables)

To make enough for 6 people: mix together 3 finely chopped garlic cloves, 1 tbsp Dijon or wholegrain mustard, 4 tbsp white-wine vinegar, 2 tbsp chopped fresh marjoram or thyme and 8 tbsp olive oil. Season well and use to coat the sausages, chops or chunks of vegetables. Leave to marinate for about 30 minutes before cooking.

Stylish pan sauces

Chasseur

After pan-frying any meat, add some chopped mushrooms and shallots to the pan with a little butter. Once softened, add half a glass of white wine and reduce the liquid by half. Add some chopped fresh herbs.

Mustard

After pan-frying pork, lamb or beef and deglazing the pan with a little white wine, add flour and butter to the pan. Cook for 1 minute, then stir in a carton of single cream, 1–2 tsp English mustard powder and 1 tsp vinegar for piquancy.

Sweet-and-sour (for stir-fries)

Make this in a separate pan from the one in which you are stir-frying. Add a wine glass of orange juice to the pan, plus 1 tbsp each of tomato purée, sherry, demerara sugar and wine vinegar. Stir over a high heat to dissolve the sugar, and thicken the sauce with 1 tsp cornflour dissolved in water.

Sablés

These home-made biscuits are great to serve with light fruity desserts, such as the summer fruit jellies or bavarois.

To make 12 biscuits: in a large bowl, mix together 85g/3oz plain flour, 25g/1oz caster sugar, 25g/1oz ground almonds and the finely grated zest of half a lemon or 1 orange. Rub in 50g/2oz butter to make fine crumbs, then mix in 1 egg yolk to form a soft dough. (You can also do this in a food processor.)

Roll out on a floured surface to a 25 x 20cm/10 x 8in rectangle, 3mm/1/8in thick. Use a pastry wheel, if you have one, to cut the dough into two strips, 10cm/4in wide, then cut the strips across at 5cm/2in intervals to make rectangular biscuits. Or cut the biscuits out with a fluted round cutter. Arrange the biscuits, slightly apart, on baking sheets. Chill for 30 minutes.

Preheat the oven to 180C/350F/Gas 4. Bake the biscuits for 10 minutes until they are very lightly browned. Leave to cool for a few minutes on the baking sheets then transfer them to a cooling rack. Dust with icing sugar to serve.

Soups

Soup is as old as the cooking pot, for as
soon as mankind learned to cook meat and
vegetables with liquid in a container, there
was good, well-flavoured soup as a by-product.
For many generations soup meant supper. The
biggest change in the soup pot for centuries
has come with our new global approach to
ingredients, techniques and flavours. Peppers,
pesto and pumpkin are now well established
in our repertoire of soups. We are as likely
to make minestrone, borscht or an Oriental
chicken noodle soup as we are to make a
deliciously familiar pea soup.

Summer minestrone soup

2 tbsp olive oil

1 small onion, finely chopped

2 celery stalks, finely chopped

1 garlic clove, chopped

850ml/1 ½ pints chicken or
  vegetable stock

225g/8oz thin asparagus, trimmed
  and cut into 1cm/½in pieces,
  using tips and tender parts

225g/8oz podded broad beans

225g/8oz young green beans, trimmed
  and cut into 1cm/½in pieces

100ml/3½fl oz single cream

50g/2oz freshly grated Parmesan
  cheese

3–4 tbsp pesto

This recipe has been adapted from one in the first *River Café
Cookbook*, and makes the most of those lovely summer vegetables.
It has been lightened, so it is ideal for a starter. This soup is so good
that you'll probably want to make it all year round, which is possible if
you use frozen beans.

1 Heat the olive oil in a large pan, then fry the onion, celery and
garlic gently for about 10 minutes until soft. Pour in the stock and
bring to the boil. Cover, lower the heat and simmer for 10–15 minutes.
2 Add the asparagus, broad beans and green beans, and cook for
5–7 minutes more until just tender.
3 Remove the pan from the heat and pour in the cream, then add the
grated Parmesan and pesto. Stir and serve.

A light, fresh Italian soup demands a light aromatic Italian white wine. Go for a Pinot Grigio or
a Frascati.

Roasted red pepper soup

Roasting peppers and tomatoes really concentrates their sweet flavour.
A roasted chilli gives a hint of hotness without being overpowering.

1 Preheat the oven to 200C/400F/Gas 6. Put the peppers and chilli, skin-side up, in one layer in a roasting tin; add the tomatoes, garlic and thyme. Drizzle with oil, season and roast for about 50 minutes until the skins are blistered and softened. Remove and discard the thyme sprigs.

2 Put the peppers in a polythene bag, seal and set aside for 15 minutes (this makes them easier to peel). Peel off the skins and put the peppers back in the tin with their juices. Peel the skin from the chilli, or scrape off the flesh into the tin. Squeeze the garlic from their skins into the tin.

3 Pour the stock into the tin and stir around to scrape up all the juices. Transfer to a blender and process until smooth. Pour into a pan and heat through. (If you need to make it thinner, just add a little more stock or water.) Season if necessary.

4 Garnish with croûtons and Parmesan shavings just before serving.

A soup bursting with flavour needs a lively young red wine, such as a Chianti or Zinfandel from Italy or California.

To prepare ahead: make up to the end of step 3, but don't garnish. Reheat gently to serve. Freeze for up to 1 month.

PREPARATION 20 MINUTES
COOKING 50–60 MINUTES
SERVES 6

4 red peppers, cored, deseeded and
    quartered
1 red chilli, halved and deseeded
450g/1lb (about 5 large) tomatoes,
    halved widthwise
2–4 garlic cloves, unpeeled
5 fresh thyme sprigs
2 tbsp olive oil
850ml/1½ pints vegetable stock
crispy garlic bread croûtons and
    Parmesan shavings (pages 16–17),
    to garnish

Cream of pumpkin soup

To prepare ahead: make up to the end of step 2, cover and chill.

PREPARATION 15–20 MINUTES
COOKING 25 MINUTES
SERVES 6

1.3kg/3lb pumpkin, peeled, sliced
  and deseeded
3 tbsp olive oil
1 large onion, chopped
2 garlic cloves, chopped
2 tsp cumin seeds
1 potato, peeled and chopped
6 fresh thyme sprigs or 1 tsp dried
700ml/1¼ pints vegetable stock
crème fraîche, to serve
deep-fried sage leaves (page 17),
  to garnish

Pumpkin, or any winter squash, gives a vibrantly coloured soup. It has a mild flavour, so a few herbs and a little toasted spice are welcome embellishments. Pumpkin is quite watery when cooked so it needs thickening; many soups suggest thickening with flour, but potato is used here.

1 Cut the pumpkin into chunks. Heat the oil in a large pan, then fry the onion, garlic and cumin for 2–3 minutes until starting to brown. Add the pumpkin and potato and fry, stirring, for 5–6 minutes. Remove the leaves from the thyme sprigs (or use dried) and sprinkle into the pan.
2 Pour in the stock and simmer for about 15 minutes until the pumpkin and potato are soft. Purée in a blender until smooth, then pour into a pan, heat through and season.
3 Serve each portion with a dollop of crème fraîche, lightly stirred in, and garnish with deep-fried sage leaves.

A warming soup with spicy notes wants a crisp, aromatic white wine; or try a dry fino sherry, which makes a great companion to many starters.

Pea and watercress soup

To prepare ahead: make up to the end of step 1, then chill for up to 1 day.

PREPARATION 5 MINUTES
COOKING 7–8 MINUTES
SERVES 4–6

1 tbsp olive oil
1 large onion, chopped
500ml/18fl oz good-quality
  vegetable stock
350g/12oz frozen peas
75g/2¾oz bag of watercress
70g/2½oz pancetta or bacon, cut
  into thin strips
oil, for frying

It was Gary Rhodes' idea to blend frozen peas after a few minutes' cooking to keep the colour.

1 Heat the olive oil in a pan, then add the onion and cook for 3–4 minutes, stirring often, until it is softened but not browned. Pour in the stock and bring to the boil, then lower the heat, add the peas and simmer for about 3 minutes.
2 Remove and discard the thicker stems from the watercress, then stir the rest into the pan. Cook for about 1 minute, then transfer to a blender and process so there is still a bit of texture. Season to taste.
3 Heat a little oil in a pan and fry the pancetta or bacon strips until crisp and golden. Remove with a slotted spoon and drain on kitchen paper. Return the soup to the pan, heat through and serve sprinkled with the crispy pancetta strips.

This needs a medium-bodied white wine, such as an unoaked Chardonnay or a Semillon/Chardonnay blend.

Borscht

To prepare ahead: make up to the end of step 3. Freeze for up to 6 months or store in the fridge for up to 1 day. Reheat gently in a pan before serving.

PREPARATION 25 MINUTES
COOKING 1½ HOURS
SERVES 6

700g/1lb 9oz raw beetroot, peeled
1 large carrot, peeled
25g/1oz butter
1 onion, very finely chopped
1 celery stalk, very finely chopped
2 large tomatoes, skinned, deseeded
  and finely chopped
2 garlic cloves, crushed
1.2 litres/2 pints hot chicken or
  vegetable stock
a few fresh parsley sprigs
1 bay leaf
2 whole cloves
1–2 tbsp lemon juice

FOR THE GARNISH
2 tsp horseradish sauce
142ml/¼ pint carton of soured cream

SOUP GARNISHES

A final flourish on top of the soup will add to its appeal, and it's a wonderful opportunity to add another texture and taste to the dish. (All the following garnishes are enough to top 6 bowls of soup.)

Garlic bread croûtons

Cut three 2cm/³/₄in thick slices from a white (preferably day-old) loaf. Cut each slice into 2cm/³/₄in cubes. Cut a garlic clove into 4 slices. Heat 3 tablespoons of olive oil in a non-stick frying pan and fry the garlic slices briefly to flavour the oil,

then remove. Fry the cubes in the oil, turning often, for 5–6 minutes until golden. Remove with a slotted spoon and drain on kitchen paper. Good on smooth puréed soups.

Potato croûtons

Peel a medium (225g/8oz) potato and cut into 1cm/½in dice. Heat 3 tablespoons of olive oil in a non-stick frying pan and add the potatoes. Fry for 7–8 minutes, turning occasionally, until golden and tender. Remove with a slotted spoon

and drain on kitchen paper. Good on spicy and vegetable soups.

Smooth pesto

Delicious stirred into soups, it's so easy to make your own pesto. Throw 5 handfuls of fresh basil into a food processor with a large pinch of salt and three halved, peeled garlic cloves. Blend to a smooth purée. Add a good handful of pine nuts and 4 tablespoons of grated Parmesan. With the motor running, add about 6–7 tablespoons of olive oil, a little at a time, until you have a smooth

There are many variations of this traditional Russian/Eastern European soup. This version is quite chunky; if you prefer it smooth, simply transfer it to a food processor and blend until smooth, or strain out the bits through a sieve. Reheat gently before serving. Borscht is traditionally served with soured cream. For an authentic favour, serve the soup with an Eastern European bread, like a rye flavoured with caraway. Borscht is just as nice served chilled in summer.

1 Grate the beetroot and carrot (pic. 1). Melt the butter in a large pan. Add the beetroot, carrot, onion and celery and cook over a moderate heat for 15 minutes, stirring occasionally until softened but not brown (pic. 2).

2 Add the tomatoes and garlic and cook for a further 10 minutes until the tomatoes are very soft.

3 Pour in the stock and season with salt and pepper. Bring to the boil. Tie the parsley, bay leaf and cloves together in a piece of muslin or new J-cloth and drop into the pan. As soon as the soup comes to the boil, cover then reduce the heat and simmer for 1 hour, stirring occasionally. Remove the bag of herbs and season with salt, pepper and lemon juice.

4 Mix together the horseradish sauce and soured cream. Ladle the soup into serving bowls, then drizzle over the horseradish soured cream.

Traditionally, the only thing to drink with Borscht is vodka. You pour a tot into the soup, then drink the rest neat. For a less intoxicating soup, choose a light, dry white wine, with enough crispness to stand up for itself. The Italian whites do the job nicely: try an unoaked Chardonnay or a Pinot Grigio. Both of these could also be drunk before the meal. Serve chilled.

texture. Taste, and season if necessary. Drizzle on to – or stir into – soups just before serving. Good on chicken and fish, and with vegetable soups.

Parsley and lemon pesto

This is a good idea for winter, using parsley as a contrast to the more summery flavour of basil. Put 4 handfuls of fresh parsley and the grated zest and juice of 1 lemon in a food processor and blend to a paste, then drizzle in enough olive oil to give a smooth consistency – about 5–6 tablespoons should be enough. Season with salt and pepper. Good on fish soups.

Deep-fried herbs

Wash a good handful of mixed herbs and dry well on kitchen paper. In a pan, heat enough oil (about 5cm/2in) to deep-fry and throw in the herbs. The oil will bubble and sizzle for about 30 seconds – as soon as the bubbling dies down, the herbs are ready. Remove with a slotted spoon and drain on kitchen paper. Deep-fry as near to serving as possible, to avoid the herbs becoming soggy. Good on thicker soups (they will sink into a thin soup).

Herb cream

Mix chopped fresh herbs with single, double or soured cream and drizzle this on to soups

just before serving. Add about 3 tablespoons of whatever herbs you like, or a mixture, to 6 tablespoons of cream. Dill and parsley are good with fish soups; sage and thyme are good with meaty or root vegetable soups. Chives work with almost anything.

Parmesan shavings

The easiest way to get attractive shavings of Parmesan cheese is to use a vegetable peeler. Start with quite a large block of Parmesan and carefully shave off thin strips. They are good on Mediterranean-flavoured soups.

Prawn bisque

To prepare ahead: make up to the end of step 2, cover and chill for up to 1 day.

PREPARATION 25 MINUTES
COOKING 50 MINUTES
SERVES 6

450g/1lb cooked prawns in their shells
1 celery stalk, chopped, plus its leaves
a few black peppercorns
50g/2oz butter
1 onion, chopped
2 carrots, chopped
1 bay leaf
3 tbsp brandy
200ml/7fl oz dry white wine
bouquet garni
about 3 tbsp basmati rice
2 tbsp tomato purée
1 tsp paprika
142ml/^{1}/$_4$ pint carton of double cream
parsley and lemon pesto (page 17),
  to garnish

This delicate bisque's subtle colour is achieved by making a stock from prawn shells. Garnishing it with parsley and lemon pesto gives it a modern twist.

1 Peel the prawns, putting the shells in a pan with the celery leaves and peppercorns. Add 1.4 litres/2^1/$_2$ pints water and bring to the boil, then reduce the heat and simmer for 30 minutes. Strain.
2 Melt the butter in another pan, then cook the onion, carrots, celery stalk and bay leaf for 7–8 minutes, stirring, until softened but not brown. Add the brandy and carefully set alight. When the flames have died down, stir in the wine. Bring to the boil, and boil rapidly for 5 minutes until reduced by half.
3 Add the prawn stock, bouquet garni, rice, tomato purée and paprika. Bring to the boil, then reduce the heat and simmer for 15 minutes until the rice is cooked. Add all but 6 of the prawns for the last 3 minutes of that time.
4 Blend the soup in batches, then pour into a pan with the cream; season. Chop the reserved prawns, then stir into the soup and heat gently. Serve drizzled with the pesto.

Use a very light, dry white wine for the cooking, then serve it with the soup. A crisp Sauvignon Blanc from the south of France will do very nicely.

Smoked haddock chowder

Make up to 4 hours ahead, without the bacon. Freeze for up to 1 month.

PREPARATION 10 MINUTES
COOKING 40 MINUTES
SERVES 6

450g/1lb natural (undyed) smoked haddock
700ml/1¼ pints milk
50g/2oz butter
1 leek, finely chopped
350g/12oz floury potatoes, such as Maris Piper, cut into 2.5cm/1in dice
8–10 slices of streaky bacon
pinch of freshly grated nutmeg
2 tbsp chopped fresh parsley
a few chive stalks

In the USA, home of fish chowder, bowls of this thick creamy soup are served as a filling lunch. Here it is lightened to serve as a starter.

1 Put the haddock and milk in a pan, bring to the boil, then cover and simmer for 10 minutes until the fish is just cooked. Using a fish slice, transfer the fish to a plate and set aside. Strain the cooking liquid and set aside.

2 Heat the butter in a large pan, then fry the leek until softened. Tip in the potatoes and cook for 5 minutes. Pour in the reserved fish cooking liquid, bring to the boil, then cover and simmer for 20 minutes. Mash a little potato against the side of the pan – this helps to thicken the soup.

3 Cut the bacon slices lengthwise into three strips each and grill until crispy. Skin and flake the fish and add to the soup with the nutmeg, black pepper and parsley. Heat for a few minutes.

4 Arrange the bacon on top of the soup with the chive stalks.

To complement the fish, this soup needs a young subtly oaked Chardonnay. A heavily oaked white would spoil the flavours.

Shredded chicken noodle soup

Make up to the end of step 1, then chill the stock and chicken separately for up to 1 day. Freeze for up to 1 month.

No stock is needed for this clear soup – the chicken creates its own as it simmers in water fragrantly spiced with ginger and garlic.

PREPARATION 15 MINUTES
COOKING 2 HOURS
SERVES 6

2 chicken legs
6 thick slices of fresh root ginger
½ tsp black peppercorns
1 tsp salt
2 garlic cloves in their skins, halved
bunch of spring onions
85g/3oz (1 strip) fine egg noodles
2 tbsp light soy sauce

TO SERVE
1 red chilli, deseeded and cut into
  thin strips
sesame oil

1 Put the chicken legs in a large pan, pour in 2.25 litres/4 pints water, bring to a simmer and let it cook very gently, without boiling, for 20 minutes, skimming occasionally, without stirring, until the stock is clear.

2 Lower the heat, add the ginger, peppercorns, salt, garlic and 4 spring onions, sliced into long pieces. Simmer for 1½ hours, skimming off any fat from time to time. Remove the chicken from the pan, then strain the stock through a fine mesh sieve into a pan. (For a crystal-clear soup, strain again through muslin.)

3 When the chicken is cool enough to handle, shred the meat and add to the stock. Bring just to the boil, add the noodles and simmer for 3 minutes.

4 Cut the remaining spring onions into fine short shreds and throw a handful into the hot soup. Warm through for a few seconds. Season with the soy sauce.

5 Serve each bowl of soup sprinkled with a few chilli strips and drizzled with sesame oil.

A good match for this soup is an Alsace Gewürztraminer. Alternatively, try a young dry Riesling from Germany or Australia.

Mushroom and duck soup

Cooking the duck breast with the soup not only adds extra texture, but also gives the broth – already enriched with porcini mushrooms – a rich gamey flavour.

1 Break the dried porcini into small pieces and soak in the boiling water for 30 minutes.
2 Heat the oil in a large pan, then cook the shallots and garlic for 1–2 minutes. Add the chestnut mushrooms and cook over a medium heat, tossing frequently, for 7–8 minutes until golden.
3 Remove and discard the duck skin and fat. Add the meat to the pan and pour over the stock. Bring to the boil, then reduce the heat. Cover and simmer for 20 minutes until the duck is just cooked.
4 Remove the duck with a slotted spoon and set aside until cool enough to handle. Using two forks, shred the duck meat quite finely and return to the pan. Add the porcini mushrooms with their liquor and the soy sauce, and season with salt and pepper. Stir in the parsley and warm through for a few minutes.

As it's wonderfully rich and intense, this soup needs a good quality medium-bodied fruity red wine, such as a Côtes-du-Rhône or a young Rioja.

To prepare ahead: make the soup but don't garnish it; cool and chill. Reheat gently before serving. Freeze for up to 1 month.

PREPARATION 15 MINUTES, PLUS
 30 MINUTES' SOAKING
COOKING 25 MINUTES
SERVES 6

10g/^{1}/$_3$oz packet of dried porcini
   mushrooms or 450g/1lb fresh porcini
   (in autumn)
450ml/^{3}/$_4$ pint boiling water
2 tbsp olive oil
2 shallots, very finely chopped
2 garlic cloves, crushed
350g/12oz chestnut mushrooms, sliced
175–200g/6–7oz duck breast
600ml/1 pint chicken stock
1 tbsp light soy sauce
3 tbsp chopped fresh parsley

Starters

The starter arrives when appetites are at their sharpest, which makes it the most important and often the most appreciated part of the meal. Indeed, there are people who regularly order two starters in a restaurant and skip the main course. Great starters make you feel happy and relaxed, because they promise good things to come. The rules are straightforward: keep compositions simple, ingredients light, colours bold, flavours strong and clearly defined. Serve a hot starter and you have the added bonus of luring your guests to the table with enticing aromas.

Garlicky mushroom toasts

To prepare ahead: make the toasts up to the end of step 1.

PREPARATION 10 MINUTES
COOKING 15 MINUTES
SERVES 6

1 tbsp olive oil
2 garlic cloves, crushed
450g/1lb mixed mushrooms, such as chestnut and oyster, sliced
3 tbsp marsala, Madeira or sweet sherry
284ml/½ pint carton of double cream

FOR THE TOASTS
1 ciabatta loaf, cut into three chunks
50g/2oz butter, softened
4 tbsp chopped fresh parsley

If you see some especially good fresh mushrooms in the greengrocer's or supermarket, snap them up for this lovely starter, which can be assembled in minutes.

1 First make the toasts: preheat the grill and split each ciabatta chunk in half. Grill on the crust sides. Mix the butter and parsley; spread over the cut sides of the ciabatta.
2 Heat the oil in a large frying pan. Add the garlic and mushrooms and fry over a fairly high heat for 6–7 minutes, turning occasionally; cook until the liquid evaporates.
3 Pour the marsala, Madeira or sherry into the pan and bubble for a few minutes. Stir in the cream; season with salt and pepper. Toast the cut side of the ciabatta until the butter is melted and golden.
4 Put the pieces of ciabatta on plates, spoon over the mushrooms and season with black pepper.

These deliciously rich and meaty mushrooms deserve much the same treatment as a good steak, so ideally team them with a good quality Rioja reserva, or an equally good French Merlot.

Mushrooms and artichokes à la Grecque

To prepare ahead: make up to 2 days ahead, stirring every so often.

PREPARATION 10 MINUTES
COOKING 2 MINUTES
SERVES 6

450g/1lb chestnut mushrooms
1 tsp coriander seeds
4 tbsp olive oil
2 tbsp fresh lemon juice
150ml/¼ pint dry white wine
280g/10oz jar of artichoke hearts in oil, drained
4 tbsp chopped fresh parsley or coriander

If chestnut mushrooms are not available, use another closed cap or large button mushroom. Try to buy similar sized ones, so the slices are evenly matched. Make this dish a couple of hours ahead to allow the flavours to develop fully. Serve with a warm, crusty, white rustic loaf.

1 Trim and slice the mushrooms and put in a large bowl. Crack the coriander seeds using a pestle and mortar or a rolling pin in a cup.
2 Put the coriander seeds in a frying pan and heat gently until aromatic. Add the oil, lemon juice, wine and salt and pepper. Bring to the boil and simmer for 2 minutes, then pour over the mushrooms and stir well.
3 Leave at room temperature, stirring occasionally, for at least 1 hour.
4 Just before serving, stir in the artichoke hearts and chopped herbs.

Pick a crisp fresh white, such as a Sauvignon Blanc or more aromatic dry Muscat.

THE RIGHT BREAD

It is often quite important to make sure that your starter and the bread you are serving are properly paired. For example, walnut bread goes well with salads and light or cheesy starters, particularly goats' cheese. French sticks may not be original, but a fresh baguette is a great accompaniment to a rich starter, such as rillettes. However, there's plenty of room for matchmaking.

Another bread of Gallic origin is fougasse, the French equivalent of Italian focaccia. Made from unbleached white flour and olive oil, both are flattish and have fingertip dents, but focaccia is sprinkled with salt crystals, so do not serve it with salty or smoked fish starters. Buy or bake on the day of serving. Italian ciabatta is ideal with cold soups, such as gazpacho, and salads. Be careful when reheating ciabatta as it dries out very quickly, and avoid ready-to-bake ones. Pan pugliese is a deeper, rounder Italian loaf with a floury finish. It is more suitable when you want to serve sliced bread with a starter.

Germany (and Eastern Europe) is the home of rye bread, which can be pale and light, or dark and dense, and contains caraway seed. Some versions contain aniseed, coriander and fennel. These strong flavours go well with cold starters such as cured or roll-mop herrings, or other oily fish, and pastrami.

The Americas are noted for their sourdough bread. It's hard to make at home but supermarkets now stock loaves from specialist bakeries. These are great with leafy salads and cold starters that require hot toast, but watch out as they are very filling. With its cake-like texture and sweet flavour, cornbread, from the southern states of America, is also popular. Its sweetness goes well with cold starters containing bacon, ham, salami, chorizo and pepperoni.

British breads can rival any opposition when baked well. Soda bread from Ireland has a pleasant gritty texture and a butter-milky taste, and must be eaten warm and fresh – make it yourself for best impressions. A crusty cottage or farmhouse loaf is ideal for buttering thickly, should that match your starter. And soft wholemeal bread is the ideal accompaniment for smoked salmon.

The popularity of Indian meals has widened our appreciation of their flat breads – paratha and chapatti (fried), and naan (baked). These breads can be plain or flavoured with garlic, coriander and cumin. They are ideal to serve with Indian-style starters that have a sauce to mop up. Plain unleavened breads from the Middle East, such as pitta, are great for serving with hummus and other dips and spreads.

Serve it warm

The aroma of freshly baked bread provides a warm welcome as guests arrive. But just-baked bread can be impossible to slice and tastes better cooled a little. Bake it in advance, then reheat it in a moderate oven just before serving, but do not leave it in for longer than 10 minutes or it will dry out, and never slice bread before reheating. Wrap warm sliced bread in a large napkin laid in a bread basket. Reheat flat breads, such as pitta and naan, under a moderate grill for 1–2 minutes on each side – sprinkle lightly with water to prevent them drying out.

Melba toast

Chic in the 70s, Melba toast is making a comeback. Lightly toast a thick slice of white bread, then cut off the crusts and slice through the centre. Put the toast, cut-side up, under a medium to hot grill and watch it go golden and its edges curl. Remove before it burns, and serve warm.

Bread accompaniments

Some of the best modern starters are simply something tasty on toast – Italian bruschetta and crostini, or French croûtes laden with pâté, antipasti or grilled cheese. When starters are not bread-based, they usually need some sort of bread to mop up sauces or simply stem guests' hunger. Something starchy and crisp can offer a good balance of texture – serve hot naan or crisp poppadom with spicy starters, prawn crackers with fishy ones, and grissini breadsticks to provide crunch with salads. The following recipes all serve 6 to 8.

Bruschetta

Hugely popular as an accompaniment or as an appetizer. Toast 6 slices of ciabatta until golden, then drizzle generously with olive oil and rub with half a cut garlic clove. Top with skinned, seeded, chopped tomatoes and freshly torn basil leaves. Drizzle with a little more oil, season and serve warm or cold.

Crisp garlic bread

Mix 50g/2oz butter with 3 finely chopped garlic cloves and a little fresh chopped parsley or snipped chives. Toast one side of 6 slices of French bread, then spread the untoasted side with the garlic butter. Grill until the butter has melted and the bread is crisp and golden.

Garlic pitta

Cut 6 pitta breads into strips and toast them lightly until they start to turn golden. Mix two finely chopped garlic cloves with melted butter or olive oil, brush liberally over the strips and serve them hot.

Special flavours

Rosemary: halfway through baking, brush both sides with olive oil. Sprinkle the top with a few fresh rosemary leaves and coarse sea salt, and finish baking.
Basil and garlic: halfway through baking, brush both sides with olive oil. Sprinkle the top with torn fresh basil leaves and a little finely chopped garlic, and finish baking.

Roast asparagus with poached egg

To prepare ahead: complete step 1 and prepare the asparagus for roasting; chill for up to 24 hours.
Store the crumbs in an airtight container for up to 24 hours.

PREPARATION 10 MINUTES
COOKING 20–25 MINUTES
SERVES 6

25g/1oz butter
50g/2oz fresh white breadcrumbs
grated zest of 1 lemon
3 tbsp chopped parsley
450g/1lb thin asparagus spears
olive oil, for brushing and drizzling
150ml/¼ pint white wine vinegar
6 very fresh eggs
Parmesan shavings, to serve

Asparagus is now available all year round, but it is at its best during the few weeks in May and June when British asparagus is in season. There's no need to peel asparagus but, if it is thick, snap off any woody stems at the point where they break easily.

1 Melt the butter in a pan and fry the breadcrumbs, stirring often, until crisp. Remove from the heat and season. Stir in lemon zest and parsley.
2 Preheat the oven to 200C/400F/Gas 6. Lay the asparagus on an oiled baking sheet and brush them with oil. Roast for 12–15 minutes.
3 Meanwhile, half-fill a medium pan with water, add the vinegar and bring to the boil. Crack in the eggs from a height of 10cm/4in (this gives them a good round shape). Simmer until the white is firm, 3–4 minutes. Using a slotted spoon, transfer to a bowl of warm water (for up to 30 minutes).
4 Arrange the asparagus on plates. Drizzle with oil and scatter over the Parmesan. Spoon the eggs on top and sprinkle with the flavoured crumbs. Season with coarse sea salt and black pepper.

Asparagus on its own appreciates a crisp Sauvignon Blanc, but the rich running egg yolk makes a difference. Instead, try serving a riper, richer unoaked Chardonnay from California or Chile.

Baba ghanoush

Make up to 3 days ahead and chill. Remove from the fridge 30 minutes before serving.

PREPARATION 20 MINUTES
COOKING 25 MINUTES
SERVES 6

3 large aubergines, about 900g/2lb
   total weight
2 garlic cloves
4 tbsp tahini paste
juice of 3 lemons (100ml/3½fl oz)
1 tsp ground cumin
handful of parsley
100g/4oz black olives, pitted
6 small tomatoes, sliced
1 small red onion, thinly sliced
olive oil, to drizzle
6 toasted pitta breads, to serve

The smoky sweet flavour of this Middle Eastern dip makes a great starter that is perfect before light dishes, or roasted fish or chicken.

1 Preheat the grill. Grill the whole aubergines, turning occasionally, for about 20–25 minutes until soft and charred. Allow to cool.
2 Trim off the stalks, cut each aubergine in half and scoop the flesh into a food processor. Add the garlic, tahini, lemon juice, cumin, parsley, and salt and pepper, and process until smooth.
3 Put a large spoonful of the baba ghanoush mixture on to each plate. Put some olives and tomato and onion slices to one side, then drizzle with a little olive oil. Sprinkle with black pepper and serve with toasted pitta.

Choose a light, fresh red wine to match this exotic dish's delicate blend of flavours. Look for southern French wines from Provence, Languedoc-Roussillon or the Rhône Valley.

Aubergine and mozzarella stacks

These Mediterranean towers will bring sunshine flavours to your dinner party at any time of year. Serve with garlic bread.

Make the stacks up to the end of step 2, then cover and chill for up to 24 hours. Make the sauce, cover and chill for up to 2 days.

PREPARATION 20 MINUTES
COOKING 20–25 MINUTES
SERVES 6

1 aubergine
about 2 tbsp olive oil
150g/5oz mozzarella
6 slices of prosciutto
handful of basil leaves, torn, to serve

FOR THE SAUCE
350g/12oz jar of passata, or 400g/14oz can of chopped tomatoes and 2 tsp tomato purée
2 tbsp extra-virgin olive oil
1 garlic clove, chopped

1 Preheat the oven to 200C/400F/Gas 6. Cut twelve 1cm/^{1}/$_2$in aubergine slices and put them over the grill pan in one layer. Brush with half the olive oil. Grill for 3–4 minutes, then turn, brush and grill again. Allow to cool.
2 Cut the mozzarella into 6 slices. Sandwich each between 2 aubergine slices and put in a greased shallow ovenproof dish. Crumple a prosciutto slice on top of each. Bake for 12–15 minutes until the cheese melts.

3 Make the sauce: put all the ingredients in a pan and simmer briefly (or until slightly thickened, if using canned tomatoes). Spoon a little sauce on each plate, put the stacks on top and scatter with basil.

This Mediterranean dish will go well with most Mediterranean reds. Try especially any of the new wave of red wines of southern Italy, from Puglia, Calabria and Sicily, which are made from local varieties and are really full of flavour.

Feta and Piedmontese peppers

Roast the peppers up to 1 day ahead, cover and chill. Remove from the fridge 30 minutes before serving.

PREPARATION 15 MINUTES
COOKING 30 MINUTES
SERVES 6

3 red peppers
85g/3oz can of anchovies in oil, drained
1 garlic clove, finely chopped
200g/7oz cherry tomatoes, quartered
2 tbsp olive oil
2 tsp balsamic vinegar
150g/5oz feta cheese
a few fresh basil leaves, shredded

The delicious roasted sweetness and the colour of the red peppers contrast brilliantly with the sharpness of the crumbly white feta. Use any colour of pepper, except green (as these are not sweet enough). As a change from feta, you could use another crumbly cheese, such as good old British Wensleydale or a sharp goats' cheese.

1 Preheat the oven to 190C/375F/Gas 5. Quarter the peppers and deseed them. Put them in one layer, skin side down, in a roasting tin. Cut the anchovies into 24 strips (you get about 10 in a can, so halve most and cut a couple of larger ones into three).
2 Mix together the garlic, tomatoes, oil and vinegar. Season with salt and pepper, then spoon a little into the cavity of each pepper. Put 2 anchovy strips in a cross on each.
3 Bake for 25–30 minutes until the peppers are tender. Leave to cool.
4 Slice the feta thinly, then break into pieces. Put 2 pepper pieces on each plate and drizzle over the pan juices. Sprinkle with the crumbled feta and shredded basil.

Stuffed peppers usually demand a full-bodied red, but here the cheese and anchovies make a better match with a crisp white Muscadet or a lightly fizzy young Vinho Verde.

Stilton pâté with celery and walnut salad

To prepare ahead: make the pâté up to the end of step 1, then chill for up to 1 week or freeze for up to 3 months.

PREPARATION 15 MINUTES
SERVES 6

225g/8oz Stilton, at room temperature, crumbled
100g/4oz full-fat soft cheese
1 tbsp port
pinch of freshly grated nutmeg
100g/4oz walnut pieces
150g/5oz black grapes, halved
4 celery stalks, thinly sliced
2 tbsp olive oil
juice of ½ lemon
4 tbsp snipped fresh chives
Melba toast (page 25), or walnut or olive bread, to serve

1 With a fork, blend the cheeses with the port and grated nutmeg and black pepper to taste. Pile the mixture on to a sheet of foil, then wrap and shape into an 18cm/7in sausage.
2 Finely chop half the walnuts. Unwrap the cheese and coat evenly with walnuts, then wrap and chill until ready to serve.
3 Mix together the grapes, celery and remaining walnuts. Put the oil and lemon juice in a screw-top jar with a little salt and pepper.

Shake well, then stir in the chives and pour over the salad. Stir well.
4 Divide the salad between 6 plates. Slice the cheese pâté into 12 slices and put 2 slices on top of each salad. Serve with toast or bread.

Why not enjoy a glass of port with the pâté? Use a tawny port, as old as you can afford. Otherwise choose a light fruity red wine from southern France.

Crab cakes with butter sauce

Subtly spiced to prime your tastebuds, these fish cakes are ideal to precede a meal with a modern blend of Asian flavours, or a poultry or meat main course.

Shape the cakes, cover and chill several hours ahead; or open-freeze on baking sheets, wrap and freeze for up to 1 month. The sauce is not suitable for freezing.

PREPARATION 10 MINUTES
COOKING 25 MINUTES
SERVES 6

225g/8oz crab meat, fresh or frozen
225g/8oz skinned cod fillet
1 tbsp nam pla (fish sauce)
1 red chilli, deseeded and chopped
grated zest of 1 small lemon
4 spring onions, chopped
1 garlic clove, roughly chopped
small handful of coriander leaves,
    chopped
1 small egg, beaten
2 tbsp groundnut or sunflower oil
salad leaves, to serve

FOR THE BUTTER SAUCE
3 tbsp white wine
3 tbsp white wine vinegar
4 black peppercorns
2 shallots, finely chopped
2 fresh parsley sprigs
1 lemon grass stalk, split and halved
225g/8oz chilled, diced unsalted butter
1 tbsp lemon juice
small handful of coriander leaves,
    chopped

1 Put the crab, cod, nam pla, chilli, lemon zest, spring onions, garlic and coriander in a food processor and process for 30 seconds. Transfer to a bowl, stir in the egg and season. Divide into 12 round cakes.
2 Heat the oil in a frying pan. Fry the cakes for 3–4 minutes on each side until lightly golden. Drain on kitchen paper and keep warm.
3 Make the sauce: put the white wine, vinegar, black peppercorns, shallots, parsley and lemon grass in a small pan. Bring to the boil and cook for 3–4 minutes to reduce by half. Strain into a clean pan, bring to the boil and then simmer. Whisk in the butter, a piece at a time, until the sauce thickens. Season, then add the lemon juice and coriander. Remove from the heat.
4 Divide the crab cakes between 6 plates. Garnish with the salad leaves and drizzle over the sauce.

Dishes with Asian spices are often matched with Gewürztraminers, but a chilled Italian Pinot Grigio or a Sauvignon Blanc will do just as well. For fuller flavour and richness, try a Chilean Sauvignon Blanc.

Creole potted prawns

Make up to the end of step 1, cover and chill for up to 24 hours. As long as the prawns have not been frozen before, make up to the end of step 1, cover and freeze for up to 1 month.

PREPARATION 5 MINUTES
COOKING 1 MINUTE
SERVES 6

350g/12oz small peeled prawns
175g/6oz unsalted butter
3 tbsp fresh lemon juice
¼ tsp cayenne pepper
good pinch of freshly grated mace
good pinch of freshly grated nutmeg
French bread, to serve

1 Pack the prawns into 6 small heatproof bowls or ramekins (each about 125ml/4fl oz capacity). In a small pan, melt the butter gently, then add the lemon juice, cayenne, mace and nutmeg. Season with salt and pepper. Pour over the prawns and leave to set, then chill until ready to serve.

2 Just before serving, toast thin slices of French bread. Heat the ramekins in the microwave on High for 30 seconds (or sit them briefly in a basin of hot water), then serve on plates with the toast.

Choose one of the white wines that classically match Asian food to counter the cayenne – Gewürztraminer, of course, or a young dry Riesling. Serve well chilled. Traditionally these are German wines, but look out for good value Australian versions.

Thai prawn salad

Make up to the point where you pour over the dressing, then chill for up to 6 hours.

PREPARATION 20 MINUTES
COOKING ABOUT 10 MINUTES
SERVES 6

85g/3oz rice noodles
150g/5oz green beans, halved
3 tbsp nam pla (fish sauce)
juice of 3 limes
2cm/¾in piece of fresh root ginger, finely chopped
1–2 tsp sugar
1 red chilli, thinly sliced
handful of chopped fresh coriander
16 large peeled cooked prawns
lime wedges, to serve

Choose a thin noodle nearest in size to vermicelli, or fine egg noodles.

1 Put the noodles in a large bowl, pour over enough boiling water to cover and set aside for 4 minutes. Drain in a colander and refresh under cold running water.

2 Cook the green beans in a pan of boiling salted water for 3–4 minutes until just tender. Drain, then plunge into a bowl of cold water to stop them cooking.

3 Meanwhile, mix together the fish sauce, lime juice, ginger, sugar and chilli. Stir in most of the coriander. Mix the prawns with the drained beans and noodles, then toss with the dressing.

4 Spoon into bowls, garnish with the remaining coriander and serve with lime wedges.

If you make this for a buffet with other dishes, why not serve a light lager like Kingfisher? Or choose an aromatic dry white wine, such as a Gewürztraminer or a young Riesling.

Individual smoked salmon pots

This excellent no-cook starter – a home-made mayonnaise mixed with capers, shallots and finely chopped smoked salmon – makes the perfect introduction to a chicken or meat dish.

To prepare ahead: make the salmon pots, not the salad, a day ahead, cover with plastic film and chill.

PREPARATION 20 MINUTES
SERVES 6

450g/1lb smoked salmon
3 egg yolks
100ml/3½fl oz olive oil
100ml/3½fl oz sunflower oil
2 tsp drained capers, very
  finely chopped
1 shallot, very finely chopped
½ cucumber
1 tbsp white wine vinegar
dill sprigs and more whole
  capers, to garnish

1 Line 6 small ramekins with plastic film. Cut 6 strips from the smoked salmon, about 2.5 x 25cm/1 x 10in. Line the side of each ramekin with a smoked salmon strip (pic. 1).
2 Blend the egg yolks and some salt and pepper in a food processor until smooth, then drizzle in the oils in a thin steady stream until the mayonnaise is smooth, thick and shiny. Tip into a bowl and stir in the capers and shallot.
3 Chop the remaining salmon and blend in the food processor (no need to wash) until roughly minced. Add 6 tablespoons of the mayonnaise (any leftover mayonnaise can be kept in a jar or covered container in the fridge for up to 1 week) and mix lightly.
4 Divide the salmon mayonnaise between the ramekins (pic. 2) and smooth down lightly. Cover with plastic film and chill for 1 hour, or overnight.
5 Cut the cucumber in half lengthwise and scoop out the seeds. Cut into long thin strips with a potato peeler (pic. 3), then put in a bowl with the vinegar and a little salt.
6 Invert each ramekin on to a small plate, remove the ramekin and peel off the plastic film. Spoon a little more mayonnaise on top of each pot and garnish with a dill sprig and two capers. Put a small pile of cucumber strips beside each and serve.

Smoked salmon demands the best – a tip-top well-chilled Chardonnay, such as Chablis, is ideal. The capers and dressing give an extra tang, but will still complement the wine.

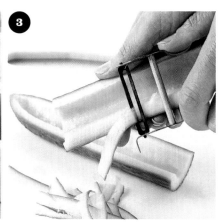

Earl Grey smoked chicken salad

It was Ken Hom's idea to use tea leaves to smoke chicken. Here the recipe is adapted to use Earl Grey, which goes very well with the fresh watercress sauce.

Start preparing the chicken up to 3 days in advance, or make the chicken up to the end of step 3, cover and freeze for up to 1 month; defrost in the fridge.

PREPARATION 15 MINUTES
COOKING 30 MINUTES
SERVES 6

5 tsp light muscovado sugar
finely grated zest and juice of 1 lemon
3 skinless chicken breast fillets
1 tbsp uncooked rice
5 tbsp Earl Grey tea leaves
150g/5oz watercress
6 tbsp crème fraîche

1 Mix 2 teaspoons of sugar with the lemon zest and a little salt and pepper. Rub over the chicken, wrap in plastic film and leave to marinate overnight.
2 Line the inside of a heavy roasting tin with foil. Put the rice, remaining sugar and tea leaves in the bottom. Rub a grill rack small enough to fit in your tin with a little oil and fit it over the smoking ingredients.
3 Heat the roasting tin on the hob. When the mixture begins to smoke, unwrap the chicken and place on the rack. Completely enclose in foil, sealing the edges. Reduce the heat to very low and smoke slowly for 30 minutes. Remove from the heat and allow to stand for 5 minutes. Remove the chicken from the tin and allow to cool completely.
4 Process a quarter of the watercress in a blender or food processor with a squeeze of lemon juice, the crème fraîche and a little salt until smooth, adding one or two teaspoons of water if it is too thick.
5 Divide the remaining watercress between 6 plates. Thinly slice the chicken and arrange over the top. Serve drizzled with the sauce.

A light wine is needed for this delicately scented dish. Choose a very restrained Pinot Grigio from northern Italy. Alternatively, serve some weak black Earl Grey in fine china cups.

Pork and duck rillettes

Make up to 3 days ahead, then chill.

PREPARATION 10 MINUTES
COOKING 2 HOURS, PLUS OVERNIGHT
    CHILLING
SERVES 10

900g/2lb boneless pork belly strips
2 duck breasts, about 300g/10oz in total
2 garlic cloves
3 fresh thyme sprigs
2 juniper berries
2 bay leaves
250ml/9fl oz white wine

TO SERVE
toasted brioche or baguette
unsalted butter
cornichons
radishes
sea salt flakes

This variation of the classic French potted meat comes up to date with a smooth, soft, heady blend of juniper, thyme, pork and duck.

1 Preheat the oven to 150C/ 300F/Gas 2. Cut the rind off the pork belly strips.
2 Put all the ingredients in a casserole with a teaspoon of salt and 100ml/3½fl oz water, cover tightly and cook for 2 hours. Allow to cool slightly, then transfer the meat to a chopping board, and strain the stock through a fine sieve.
3 Using two forks, shred the meat and fat into fine strips and pack into a bowl. Mix the meats well. Taste the stock and add salt if needed. Level the top of the meat and press lightly. Pour the stock over the meat until just covered. Cover with plastic film and chill overnight until the stock is set.
4 Cut the rillettes into rough slices and serve with the brioche or baguette, butter, cornichons, radishes and sea salt.

This famous dish deserves a famous wine. Pick a good white – Tokay Pinot Gris from Alsace is a delicious choice – or choose a top-quality Sauvignon Blanc.

Chicken liver salad

To prepare ahead: cook and marinate the vegetables. Prepare the chicken livers, cover and chill until ready to cook.

PREPARATION 15 MINUTES, PLUS
    1 HOUR'S MARINATING
COOKING 45 MINUTES
SERVES 6

8 shallots, halved
300g/10oz baby beetroot, trimmed
4 tbsp olive oil
4 tbsp groundnut or sunflower oil
2 tbsp sherry vinegar or wine vinegar
½ tsp caster sugar
300g/10oz chicken livers, rinsed and
    patted dry, cut into bite-sized pieces
225g/8oz baby spinach leaves

Beetroot adds a sweetly delicate flavour and vibrant colour to this starter. If you can't get baby beetroot, use two larger ones, peeled and cut into small chunks.

1 Preheat the oven to 200C/400F/Gas 6. Put the shallots and beetroot in a roasting tin. Drizzle with 2 tablespoons of olive oil and season. Cook for 40 minutes until tender.
2 In a large bowl, mix the rest of the olive oil with 2 tablespoons of groundnut or sunflower oil, the vinegar and sugar. Season and set this dressing aside.
3 Cut the beetroot in half and add to the bowl with the shallots. Mix well and leave to marinate for 1 hour.
4 Heat the remaining oil in a pan, add the livers and fry, stirring, for 4–5 minutes until tinged brown.
5 Put the spinach on plates, top with some livers and spoon over the beetroot and shallots. Drizzle with the dressing to serve.

Match the soft sweetness of the chicken livers and beetroot to a light fruity red such as a Beaujolais or a vin de pays d'Oc.

Lunches & light meals

Naturally, entertaining doesn't always need to
entail a dinner party of three or four courses.
Increasingly nowadays, you often want simply
to give friends an informal lunch after a
shopping expedition or a light supper before
or after a visit to the theatre or cinema. All the
dishes in this chapter are designed to provide
just such light but satisfying meals. Many of
them make excellent quick snacks and most
only require the addition of good bread, perhaps
an accompanying salad and a good bottle of
wine, to make a meal that you and your
guests will want to linger over and remember.

Tomato and dolcelatte calzone

Make the pizza base up to 2 hours ahead; chill in a bowl to slow the rising of the dough.

PREPARATION 30 MINUTES, PLUS
   20 MINUTES' RISING
COOKING 10 MINUTES
SERVES 4 (EASILY DOUBLED)

280–290g/10oz packet of pizza base mix, or pizza-and-bread mix
250ml/9fl oz hand-hot water
2 tbsp olive oil

FOR THE FILLING
4 tbsp sun-dried tomato paste
6 ripe tomatoes, skinned, deseeded and roughly chopped
300g/10oz dolcelatte cheese
175g/6oz watercress, leaves stripped from thick stems
a little milk
fresh green salad, to serve

A calzone is a pizza that has been flipped before cooking to enclose the filling. When you cut it open, the cheese will be melting and creamy.

1 Make up the pizza base mix or bread mix, adding the water and oil together. Knead for 5 minutes. Cover in a bowl until ready.
2 Divide the dough into 8 pieces and roll 4 of these into 18cm/7in rounds (keep the rest covered). Put each round on a piece of oiled foil on baking sheets. Spread each one with ½ tablespoon of the sun-dried tomato paste, leaving a 1cm/½in border.
3 Divide the tomatoes between the rounds. Roughly slice the cheese, arrange on top, then top with the watercress leaves and season. Brush the clear edges with milk.
4 Roll the other dough pieces into 18cm/7in rounds. Spread with tomato paste, leaving a 1cm/½in border. Place each one over a filled dough circle, paste side down; press around the edges to seal them well. Cover each calzone loosely with oiled plastic film and leave in a warm place for about 20 minutes.
5 Preheat a barbecue or griddle pan until really hot; oil the grid or pan well. Cook the calzone in batches for 2–3 minutes on each side. Serve with salad.

A light, chilled Valpolicella is the ideal choice – look for 'classico' for better quality; or, if the sun is shining, chill out with an Italian beer, such as Peroni, straight from the fridge.

Goats' cheese salad with roasted vegetables

To prepare ahead: roast the vegetables and cook the lentils earlier in the day.

PREPARATION 20 MINUTES
COOKING 40 MINUTES
SERVES 6 AS A MAIN COURSE SALAD

1 large aubergine, sliced
2 yellow peppers, deseeded and sliced
3 plum tomatoes, halved
4 tbsp olive oil
150g/5oz Puy lentils, rinsed
1 red onion, halved
1 carrot, quartered
2 bay leaves
bunch of fresh thyme sprigs
bunch of fresh parsley
2 tbsp balsamic vinegar
6 tbsp extra-virgin olive oil
3 firm goats' cheeses (each about 100g/4oz), halved
bag of mixed salad leaves

This salad is full of contrasting textures and flavours. Warm vegetables and green lentils are lightened by herbs and salad, with the cheese melting on top. The beauty of Puy lentils is that they don't need soaking, they cook quickly and they keep their shape.

1 Preheat the oven to 220C/425F/Gas 7. Brush the aubergine, peppers and tomatoes with olive oil. Roast on dry baking sheets for 30 minutes, turning once.
2 Put the lentils in a pan with half the onion, the carrot, bay leaves and a few herb sprigs. Cover with water, bring to the boil, cover and simmer for 25 minutes. Drain; remove the onion, carrot and herbs.
3 Whisk the vinegar and extra-virgin olive oil together. Add half of this to the lentils. Chop the remaining onion and add this to the lentils with 2 teaspoons of thyme leaves and 3 tablespoons of chopped parsley.
4 Bake the cheeses on a baking sheet for 8 minutes.
5 Meanwhile, peel the peppers, then put the vegetables, leaves and lentils on plates. Add the cheese and dressing just before serving.

Balance these rustic flavours with a red from the Côtes du Rhône. These distinctive wines are well structured, with plenty of fruit, making them ideal to serve with food.

Goats' cheese and onion tarts

For this recipe you need a firm goats' cheese that slices easily. Try Capricorn Somerset, which is widely available in supermarkets and has a gorgeous milky flavour. These tarts can be assembled ahead of time and frozen, and baked when needed (see below).

Prepare up to the point of baking the tarts in step 3; cover and chill for up to 3–4 hours before baking. Alternatively, open-freeze on baking sheets, then wrap in foil and freeze for up to 3 months. To cook, first defrost on baking sheets for 2 hours.

PREPARATION 20 MINUTES
COOKING 35 MINUTES
SERVES 6

2 red onions, thinly sliced
5 tbsp olive oil
1 tbsp balsamic vinegar
250g/9oz packet of puff pastry,
   defrosted if frozen
2 firm goats' cheeses (each about
   100g/4oz), at room temperature
125g/4½oz bag of curly endive
50g/2oz chopped walnuts
2 tsp fresh lemon juice

1 Preheat the oven to 220C/425F/Gas 7. Fry the onions gently in 2 tablespoons of the oil for 10 minutes. Add the vinegar, salt and pepper, and cook for 5 minutes until just caramelized.
2 Roll out the pastry and trim to a 20 x 30cm/8 x 12in rectangle. Cut that into six 10cm/4in squares. Put on a damp baking sheet and score lightly 1cm/½in inside each square. Do not cut through.
3 Spread the onions within this area. Use a serrated knife to cut off the ends of the cheeses and slice each into 3. Put a slice on each tart and bake for 20 minutes until the pastry puffs up.
4 Toss the endive with the walnuts, lemon juice, remaining oil, salt and pepper. Serve with the tarts.

Here is a dish that goes with both red and white wine. Choose young, light wines from the Loire, such as Chinon (red) or Sancerre (white).

Caesar salad in a Parmesan crust

For a new twist on an old favourite, add creamy avocado and crunchy pine nuts for a terrific blend of textures. The Parmesan crusts are amazingly easy to make.

Make the dressing, toast the pine nuts and make the croûtons up to 1 day ahead. Assemble just before serving.

PREPARATION 20 MINUTES
COOKING ABOUT 30 MINUTES
SERVES 6

150g/5oz Parmesan cheese, grated
4 anchovy fillets, roughly chopped
1 garlic clove, crushed
7 tbsp olive oil
2 slices of white bread
2 tsp wholegrain mustard
1 tsp sugar
1 tbsp white wine vinegar
dash of Worcestershire sauce
1 tbsp crème fraîche
1 large Cos lettuce, torn into bite-sized
  pieces
25g/1oz pine nuts, toasted
1 large avocado, cut into 1cm/$\frac{1}{2}$in
  cubes

1 Preheat the oven to 200C/400F/Gas 6. Line 2 baking sheets with non-stick baking parchment. Spoon the Parmesan on to the baking sheets in 6 evenly sized 10cm/4in rounds, with room for spreading. Bake for 8 minutes until golden. Allow to cool for 30 seconds, then remove with a palette knife and mould each around an upturned small bowl or glass to create a bowl shape. Leave to cool completely.
2 Mix the anchovies, garlic and 2 tablespoons of the oil to a paste and spread over the bread. Cook on a baking sheet for 20 minutes until crisp, then cut into 1cm/$\frac{1}{2}$in pieces; allow to cool.
3 Whisk together the mustard, sugar and vinegar. Gradually whisk in the remaining oil. Whisk in the Worcestershire sauce and crème fraîche. Season.
4 Toss the lettuce with the pine nuts, avocado and dressing. Put a Parmesan crust on each plate and spoon in the salad. Sprinkle over the anchovy croûtons.

When Caesar Gardini made his salads in Tijuana, Mexico, his customers were Americans seeking strong liquor in Prohibition days. Choose something lighter, like a Muscadet or a Beaujolais.

Parmesan soufflés with almond and anchovy sauce

People often fight shy of cooking soufflés for dinner parties, but these can be made up to 2 hours ahead – just pop them in the oven while you serve the pre-dinner drinks. If your timings miss and they are ready too soon, return them to the oven for another 5–8 minutes and they'll puff right up again.

To prepare ahead: make the soufflés up to the end of step 3. Divide between the dishes, cover and set aside in a cool place for up to 2 hours before cooking. Make the sauce the day before, then cover and chill.

PREPARATION 25 MINUTES
COOKING 25 MINUTES
SERVES 6

50g/2oz butter, plus more for greasing
85g/3oz Parmesan cheese, finely grated
50g/2oz plain flour
300ml/½ pint milk
4 eggs, separated
2 tsp Dijon mustard
pinch of cayenne pepper

FOR THE SAUCE
2 tbsp finely chopped fresh mint leaves
8 anchovy fillets, roughly chopped
25g/1oz ground almonds
6 tbsp olive oil
squeeze of lemon juice

1 Preheat the oven to 190C/375F/Gas 5. Grease 6 ramekins or individual soufflé dishes (about 200ml/7fl oz) with butter and put a teaspoon of Parmesan in each. Turn it around, tapping the dish until evenly coated.
2 Melt 50g/2oz butter in a pan over a moderate heat, stir in the flour and cook for 1 minute, stirring. Remove from the heat and gradually add the milk, stirring. Return to a moderate heat and stir until thick and silky smooth. Simmer gently for 2 minutes, then cool slightly.
3 Beat in the egg yolks, mustard, remaining Parmesan, cayenne, and salt and pepper (pic. 1). In a clean bowl, whisk the egg whites until stiff and dry. Fold a quarter into the sauce, then fold in the rest (pic. 2), cutting through and turning until evenly mixed (pic. 3).
4 Divide the mixture between the ramekins and bake for 15–20 minutes until risen and golden.
5 Meanwhile, make the sauce: put half the mint, the anchovies and almonds in a processor and blend until smooth. Add the oil and 4 table-spoons of water alternately, a tablespoon at a time, whizzing until thick. Add lemon juice and season if necessary (anchovies are very salty).
6 Put each dish on a plate and serve the sauce scattered with mint.

VARIATIONS
Once you've mastered this recipe, why not experiment? Reduce the Parmesan to 50g/2oz and add one of the following with the egg yolks: 100g/4oz small peeled, cooked prawns; 100g/4oz spinach, cooked, well drained and finely chopped; 85g/3oz chopped Brie or dolcelatte.

The anchovy sauce demands a young red wine such as a Valpolicella or a Rioja, as would a soufflé made with spinach. For a cheese soufflé, choose a French Cabernet Sauvignon; for a seafood soufflé choose an Alsace Pinot Gris or a French Chardonnay.

Prawn and crab tagliatelle

To prepare ahead: peel the prawns and prepare up to the end of step 1.

PREPARATION 30 MINUTES
COOKING 20 MINUTES
SERVES 6

125ml/4fl oz olive oil
100g/4oz smoked ham (1 thick slice), diced
1 small onion, finely chopped
2 tsp paprika
1 red pepper, deseeded and sliced
3 garlic cloves, finely chopped
a few sprigs of fresh thyme
500g/1lb 2oz egg tagliatelle
450g/1lb headless raw prawns, peeled
200g/7oz fresh crab meat (or frozen, defrosted)
1 tbsp tomato purée
1 tsp Tabasco sauce
3 tbsp chopped fresh parsley
lemon wedges, to serve

Adding fresh prawns and crab to pasta gives a stylish touch to an informal supper dish. It is worth seeking out raw prawns for the best flavour and texture.

1 Heat 2 tablespoons of the oil in a frying pan. Cook the ham and onion in it for 5 minutes until the onion has softened. Add the paprika and cook for 1 minute, then add the red pepper, garlic and thyme. Cook for 4 minutes until the pepper has just begun to soften.
2 Cook the pasta in a large pan of boiling salted water until just tender but still firm to the bite, 6–7 minutes.
3 Add the prawns to the frying pan and cook for 5 minutes, stirring until pink. Stir in the crab meat, tomato purée and 2 tablespoons of the pasta water. Season and heat through for 1–2 minutes. Remove the thyme sprigs, stir in the Tabasco and parsley, and drizzle over the remaining oil.
4 Drain the pasta, toss with the sauce and serve with lemon wedges.

Sauvignon Blanc is a good foil to this lightly spiced dish. Choose a Chilean one for fruity richness, or a New Zealand one for crisper elegance.

Fish salad with lemon basil dressing

To prepare ahead: marinate the salmon for up to 1 hour in the fridge.

These delicate summery flavours are perfect for a leisurely lunch. Serve with some warm herb bread and a bottle of chilled white wine.

PREPARATION 15 MINUTES
SERVES 6 AS A MAIN-COURSE SALAD

400g/14oz large peeled cooked
  prawns (peeled weight)
200g/7oz smoked salmon slices
2 tsp finely grated zest and the juice of
  1 large lemon (4 tbsp)
generous handful of basil leaves
2 tbsp chopped fresh parsley
125g/4^1/$_2$oz bag of mixed salad
4 spring onions
^{1}/$_2$ cucumber
250g/9oz cherry tomatoes

FOR THE LEMON BASIL DRESSING
5 tbsp light olive oil
1 tsp finely grated zest and juice of
  1 large lemon (4 tbsp)
generous handful of basil leaves

1 Put the prawns and salmon in a shallow dish. Add the lemon zest and juice, with the basil and parsley. Season and toss together. Leave to marinate while you prepare the rest of the salad.
2 Make the dressing: mix together the oil, lemon zest and juice and the basil; season.
3 Tip the salad leaves into a bowl. Slice the spring onions at an angle. Cut the cucumber into thin pieces, preferably using a mandolin grater. Add the cucumber, spring onions and tomatoes to the salad, then toss with the dressing.
4 To serve, put a pile of the mixed salad on each plate and top with the marinated salmon and prawns.

Pick one of the classic white wines for fish: a Muscadet sur lie; a good white Bordeaux; a Pinot Grigio. All of these have the freshness and style to complement the salad.

Griddled salmon with tomatoes

The dressing and the sliced salmon can be covered and chilled for up to 24 hours, while the potatoes will keep in water with a squeeze of lemon juice for up to 24 hours; drain before cooking.

PREPARATION 20 MINUTES
COOKING 10–15 MINUTES
SERVES 6

6 tbsp olive oil
2 tbsp white wine vinegar
8 coriander seeds, lightly crushed
200g/7oz cherry tomatoes, halved, deseeded and roughly chopped
6 tbsp roughly torn basil
300g/10oz new potatoes, thinly sliced
650g/1lb 7oz salmon fillet, skinned
sunflower oil, for brushing

Thinly sliced salmon cooks in seconds on a hot griddle. Serve on sliced new potatoes, tomatoes and basil, and dress with a herb vinaigrette.

1 Put the oil, vinegar and coriander seeds in a small pan and heat briefly to infuse. Toss in the tomatoes and basil, season with salt and pepper and set aside.
2 Cook the sliced potatoes in a pan of boiling salted water for about 5–8 minutes until just tender.
3 Put the salmon on a chopping board and cut at an angle into 1cm/¹/₂in thick slices. Season with salt and pepper. Brush a griddle or large frying pan with sunflower oil and heat until very hot. Then fry the salmon for about 20 seconds on each side until just cooked; keep warm.
4 Drain the potatoes and arrange on 6 plates. Top each serving with 2 salmon slices. Gently warm the sauce and drizzle it over and around the salmon and potatoes. Serve at once.

Given the tomatoes in the sauce, Sauvignon Blanc is the best match for this griddled salmon dish. These days some of the best value wines are coming from Chile, or try a Sauvignon Blanc blend from Spain.

FRYING AND GRIDDLING

Stir-frying tonight? Then get organized. Guests will love the fresh flavours and textures of a stir-fry, but they won't want you to be slicing vegetables as soon as they arrive. Stir-fries are often avoided when cooking for friends for this reason. It's a shame, because this type of cooking produces some of the healthiest, tastiest and most stylish food.

The clever combination of sweet and sour ingredients in stir-fry sauces allows complex flavours to be achieved in a short cooking time. Using a high heat also allows alcohol, such as sherry or sake, to be reduced to a delicious sauce in a very short time.

All the slicing and chopping can be done ahead so you need only toss the ingredients together and cook them at the last minute as your guests sit down. This sort of brief cooking over a high heat demands top-quality ingredients – only the most tender cuts of meat, the freshest fish and the juiciest vegetables will be able to take the pace.

Get ahead
Slice all the vegetables beforehand, then store in an airtight container, or wrap in plastic film and chill. Measure out all the sauce ingredients and mix, if required. Pre-slice or chop meat or fish, cover and chill. Lay out all the equipment you need in the kitchen ready for action. Weigh out accompaniments such as rice, couscous, noodles and pasta.

Essential equipment
Buy the deepest WOK you can, and buy larger than you think you'll need so the food does not spill out when stirring and tossing. Slightly heavier woks made of carbon steel or cast iron will conduct heat better than lighter aluminium woks.

A round-bottomed wok will need a metal ring or frame for it to remain steady on a conventional hob or when steaming. A flat, wide SPATULA enables food at the base of the wok to be reached and large quantities to be turned quickly during cooking.

Choose the right size FRYING PAN to suit the quantities of food you cook most often. The base must sit flat on the hob and be thick enough not to warp under heat stress, but make sure it's not too heavy to handle. Pans made from lighter materials will not be as durable.

Non-stick finishes are good but not essential. A well-fitting lid is a bonus for steaming or sealing. Choose a pan with a heatproof handle, but beware of wooden handles if you want to use the pan under the grill or in the oven.

GRIDDLES need to be heavy and flat so they heat up quickly, retain the heat, and do not buckle. Ridged griddles allow cooking with minimum fat. If used at a very high heat, the ridges can give an attractive cross-hatched charred appearance to food. A smooth griddle is better for pancakes and drop scones.

Secrets of success
Successful frying and griddling relies on having good-quality frying pans that will retain heat well for even cooking. Always preheat the pan, griddle or wok so that food cooks from the very moment it enters the pan. This will seal in moisture, caramelizing the food to give depth of flavour and a crispy texture to lightly cooked stir-fries – and, from longer exposure, a more heavily cooked, crispy skin on some meats and fish. Cooking at the right temperature is also the reason you get that characteristic browning of chargrilled food.

When stir-frying, keep food on the move as it cooks. The food cooks for a short time and needs careful watching, turning and timing. Don't tip all the ingredients into the pan if they are of different textures and thicknesses – those that take longer to cook go in first.

A well seasoned wok, pan or griddle (see below) will heat up without developing a blackened surface and resultant specks on the food. Once a pan has been seasoned it will have a relatively non-stick surface and will need less oil, or other fat, for cooking. This has both health and flavour benefits. To season your pan: first remove all the protective oil that covers a new wok or griddle by washing (not scouring) in very hot soapy water. Dry and put on a low heat. Wipe a little cooking oil over the inside of the wok, then heat slowly for 15 minutes; wipe again. Repeat several times until the paper is clean.

Which oil?
The most popular oil in Chinese wok cooking is groundnut oil (also known as peanut oil). Usually only small amounts of groundnut oil are needed for stir-frying. Corn oil is suitable for Chinese cooking because it has a high smoking point. Sunflower, safflower and soya bean oil may also be used – because they are higher in polyunsaturates they have a lower smoking point than groundnut and corn oil. Olive oil is more likely to feature in fusion-style dishes than conventional Oriental stir-fries – it can be used, but it does smoke more easily.

Sesame seed oil is a thicker, darker oil with a very strong flavour and a low smoking point, so add it at the end of cooking as a flavouring.

Whichever oil you use, it can be flavoured before adding the main ingredients to the pan. Once the oil is hot, but not smoking, add crushed garlic or ginger, or diced chilli, or shallots or a spice mixture, and cook very quickly, but do not allow garlic to brown as this will give a bitter flavour. If it does start to brown, remove from the wok before adding the main ingredients.

Mexican beef tortillas

These wonderfully tender beef strips wrapped in a soft tortilla with avocado, shredded lettuce and soured cream are great for informal entertaining.

To prepare ahead: marinate the beef the day before.

PREPARATION 10–15 MINUTES, PLUS AT
  LEAST 2 HOURS' MARINATING
COOKING 40 MINUTES
SERVES 6

700–900g/1lb 2oz–2lb skirt of beef
  or rump steak
3 shallots, finely chopped
300ml/½ pint red wine
4 tbsp red wine vinegar
3 tbsp olive oil
12 soft flour tortillas
2 avocados
2 tbsp lemon juice
shredded Cos lettuce
284ml/½ pint carton of soured cream

1 Well ahead, ideally the day before, put the beef in a shallow non-metallic dish. Sprinkle with the shallots, then pour over the wine, vinegar, olive oil and plenty of salt and pepper. Turn the meat in the marinade to coat, then leave for at least 2 hours or overnight.
2 Lift the beef from the marinade and put straight on to an oiled grill or hot barbecue. Cook for 10–12 minutes on each side for medium-rare. Remove, cover with foil and leave to rest for 10 minutes. Warm the tortillas for 1–2 minutes.
3 Halve the avocados, stone and peel them and then slice. Quickly toss the slices in the lemon juice and season. Slice the meat thinly across the grain.
4 Put some lettuce, avocado, beef strips and soured cream on each tortilla, then wrap into a cone.

Pick a young fruity red without bold tannins. A Spanish Tempranillo (one of the classic grapes of Rioja) delivers the berry fruit and flavour; use it for the marinade, too.

Thai beef salad

Hot, sour and sweet flavours combine in this light but satisfying Thai-style salad. A bowl of noodles, dressed with sesame oil, could be served on the side. You need 3 to 4 limes for this recipe. To get every last drop of juice, first halve the limes, then place them in a dish, cut-side down. Microwave on High for 30–45 seconds and then squeeze.

Cook the beef 1–2 hours in advance, allow to cool, then wrap in foil and keep in the fridge. Make the dressing without the fresh herbs; wash the lettuce and store in the fridge.

PREPARATION 20 MINUTES
COOKING 7 MINUTES
SERVES 6 AS A MAIN-COURSE SALAD

650g/1lb 7oz piece of fillet steak
$^{1}/_{2}$ cucumber
12 radishes, thinly sliced
150g/5oz fresh beansprouts
1 Cos lettuce

FOR THE DRESSING
6 tbsp fresh lime juice
4 tbsp nam pla (fish sauce)
1 small red chilli, finely chopped
  (deseeded if you prefer it milder)
2 tsp light muscovado sugar
2 garlic cloves, finely chopped
4 tbsp chopped fresh coriander
2 tbsp chopped fresh mint

1 Preheat a griddle pan. Season the beef with pepper and cook for 5–7 minutes, turning once, until it is cooked on the outside but still pink in the middle. Leave to rest for 15 minutes, then slice thinly.
2 Make the dressing: mix together the lime juice, fish sauce, chilli, sugar and garlic. Stir in the herbs.
3 Using a vegetable peeler, shave the cucumber into long thin strips. Mix with the beef, radishes and beansprouts. Stir in the dressing.
4 Arrange the smaller lettuce leaves on 6 plates. Tear the larger ones into pieces and add to the ingredients in the bowl. Spoon the salad on to the plates and garnish with coriander.

A fruit-driven Sauvignon Blanc makes a great match if you decide against chilled Singha beer. Choose a wine from New Zealand, Chile or Argentina.

Fish & seafood main courses

Fish and seafood are frequently looked upon as restaurant treats, like fresh cod flaking into big, juicy chunks, a silky Dover sole or a meaty crab. So why are we so reticent about cooking such delights at home? Staring fishy eyes or a strange appearance, plus the thought of complex preparation, can put people off buying. However, a good fishmonger has your interests at heart. He or she will gut, fillet, skin, slice and chop so that you don't have to. Rules, if there are any with fish, are easy: buy it fresh, keep the cooking simple and the flavourings few.

Thai seafood casserole

Chop the vegetables and spices up to an hour ahead. Freeze up to 3 months without the coriander (and rice). Thaw overnight in the fridge and reheat gently to avoid overcooking the fish.

PREPARATION 30 MINUTES
COOKING 25–30 MINUTES
SERVES 6

350g/12oz sticky rice
2 tbsp sunflower oil
9 shallots, halved
1 long red chilli, deseeded and sliced
3 garlic cloves, finely chopped
2.5cm/1in piece of fresh root ginger, chopped
225g/8oz green beans
600ml/1 pint fish stock
1 tbsp red Thai curry paste
3 fresh or dried kaffir lime leaves
700g/1lb 9oz cod or monkfish, skinned and cut into 2.5cm/1in pieces
450g/1lb raw prawns in their shells
4 tomatoes, peeled, deseeded and cut into large chunks
200g/7oz carton of coconut cream
good handful of coriander leaves

Prawns and cod, or monkfish if you are feeling extravagant, are cooked in a fragrant cream to make a delicate casserole. Serve it in large bowls or soup plates.

You can get sticky rice, Thai curry paste, kaffir lime leaves and coconut cream from ethnic stores and larger supermarkets. Use Thai fragrant rice if you can't get sticky rice.

1 Soak the rice in water for 30 minutes, then drain and cook in boiling, lightly salted water for 10–12 minutes. Drain, don't rinse.
2 Heat the oil in a flameproof casserole or shallow pan and fry the shallots until golden. Add the chilli, garlic and ginger and fry for 1 minute. Stir in the beans and fry for a further minute.
3 Stir in the stock, Thai curry paste and lime leaves. Add the fish, prawns and tomatoes and bring to the boil. Reduce the heat, cover and simmer for 5 minutes, then stir in the coconut cream and cook for 15 minutes until the fish is tender.
4 Stir in the coriander and serve with the sticky rice.

Chilled Singha beer, the Thai brand, is a great choice to cool the heat of this spicy dish, and the fizz of the beer cuts through the richness of the coconut cream.

Stir-fried seafood tagliatelle

Tagliatelle, pak choi, scallops and prawns – fabulous if cooked until just tender, not so good if overcooked by even a few minutes. This is a dish to be prepared for.

PREPARATION 20 MINUTES

COOKING 10 MINUTES

SERVES 6

300g/10oz fresh scallops with corals

300g/10oz raw prawns, defrosted if frozen

400g/14oz tagliatelle

300g/10oz pak choi leaves or shredded Chinese leaves

1 tbsp groundnut oil

125g/4¹⁄₂oz packet of cubed pancetta

1 garlic clove, chopped

1 shallot, finely chopped

200ml/7fl oz dry white wine

250ml/9fl oz double cream

1 tbsp fresh lemon juice

1 Wash the scallops and pat them dry; shell and devein the prawns.

2 Cook the pasta in boiling salted water according to the packet instructions until just tender but still firm, adding the pak choi for the last 30 seconds or so (Chinese leaves will need about 1 minute). Drain.

3 Meanwhile, heat the oil in a large frying pan and fry the pancetta for 2–3 minutes until starting to brown. Add the seafood and stir for 2 minutes until the scallops are firm and the prawns are pink. Remove the seafood and pancetta with a slotted spoon; keep warm.

4 Add the garlic and shallot to the pan and fry for 2 minutes. Add the wine and simmer, then bubble until reduced by half. Stir in the cream and lemon juice.

5 Add the fish and pancetta to the cream to heat through gently, and season.

6 Divide the tagliatelle and greens between 6 plates and top with the seafood sauce.

Match this shellfish dish with a really good white Burgundy. The acidity will balance the double cream, and the fruit will bring out the sweetness of the fish.

Cod with golden mash and sherry sauce

Cod and mash is a simple idea, but a lovely thick fillet balanced on
green beans, with a drizzling of sherry sauce, takes some beating.

1 Preheat the oven to 250C/475F/Gas 9. Make the sauce: melt half
the butter in a saucepan over a moderate heat and fry the onion for
5 minutes. Stir in the sherry and stock, and bubble until reduced by
half. Whisk in the crème fraîche and the remaining butter. Set aside
in a warm place.

2 Cook the fish: heat the olive oil and butter in a large heavy-based
roasting tin on the hob until foaming. Season the fillets and cook,
skin-side down, for 2 minutes. Turn the fillets and transfer the pan
to the oven. Cook for 3–4 minutes until just tender.

3 Reheat the sauce, add the spring onions and serve with the fish,
beans and mash.

Make the mash and sauce in advance.
Reheat the mash in the microwave,
gently reheat the sauce in a pan.

Continue the sherry theme and match this with a glass of chilled dry fino sherry; or complement
the creamy richness with a glass of Chablis.

PREPARATION 25 MINUTES

COOKING ABOUT 30 MINUTES

SERVES 6

1 tbsp olive oil

25g/1oz butter

6 skinned cod fillet pieces, each about
  175g/6oz

FOR THE SHERRY SAUCE

25g/1oz unsalted butter

1 small onion, finely chopped

150ml/^{1}/$_4$ pint medium sherry

150ml/^{1}/$_4$ pint fish stock

3 tbsp crème fraîche

2 spring onions, chopped

steamed green beans and Golden
  mash (page 111), to serve

Buy the best fish

Ask your fishmonger if he will take special orders and prepare fish for you. Supermarkets pride themselves on their wet fish counters, but often staff are not as knowledgeable as they should be and don't always have time to gut and fillet. Place special orders in advance.

It is always better to choose a whole fish if you can – once it has been filleted, fish starts to oxidize, so you may lose out on flavour. A fresh fish will be bright, shiny and firm, with bright eyes and pink or red gills, and above all should not smell fishy. Fillets and steaks should have shiny translucent flesh. Shellfish should smell of sea breezes, not fishy.

Keep an open mind when buying fish – for example, if the cod you wanted doesn't look as fresh as the haddock, take the haddock; or buy your fish first, then choose your recipe.

How much to buy?

Generally, for main course servings, per person: whole fish 350–450g/12oz–1lb; fillets and steaks 175–225g/6–8oz; shellfish (in their shells) 175–225g/6–8oz.

Keeping it fresh

Keep fish as cool and moist as possible for as short a time as you can – 24 hours at the most, in a dish covered with plastic film in the coldest part of the fridge. Whole fish keep slightly longer than fillets, but in any case keep all fish well covered in the fridge.

If you know the fish is really fresh, it can be frozen. Firm white-fleshed fish can be frozen for 3 months, but you should freeze thinner, frailer fish for no more than a couple of weeks. Oily fish keep for no more than 2 months in the freezer. Fresh mackerel, for example, is best eaten as soon after buying or catching as possible. Wrap fish well for freezing and label it. To defrost, loosen the plastic film or freezer bag and put the fish into the fridge.

Essential equipment

Top priority is a FISH FILLETING KNIFE. Even if you tend to leave all the filleting to the fishmonger, you'll find these thin-bladed, flexible knives invaluable for skinning fish and testing to see if it is cooked. For cutting tails and fins, a good strong pair of KITCHEN SCISSORS proves very useful. If you prepare lots of whole fish, look in a kitchen shop for special FISH TWEEZERS (this design is hard to miss). They have a firm grip, to tackle those bones. A FISH SCALER is another useful tool for whole fish. This can be just a short blunt knife, or have a rough grating surface.

If you want to get into cooking whole fish in a big way, invest in a FISH KETTLE, but if you haven't got the storage space, or think you'll only poach salmon or trout a couple of times a year, ask your local cookshop or fishmonger about hiring one. A specially shaped, heavy-based FISH FRYING PAN is worth considering if you like cooking whole fish. Flipping fish fillets over in the frying pan calls for a good FISH SLICE. The best ones have a thin edge and flexibility. They should be capable of safely carrying a whole cooked fish from pan to plate. There are various sizes available, so make sure you choose one that fits your pan. GRIDDLE PANS are also excellent for cooking whole fish such as sea bass or mackerel.

Skin and bones

The fashion at the moment is to keep the skin on fish fillets and cook it until it is really brown and crisp, making it a delicious feature of the recipe. Keeping the skin on helps keep the flesh together, so it doesn't break up so easily during grilling or frying.

It is sometimes easier to skin fish after it has been cooked, as it will just peel off, but removing the skin from raw fish isn't difficult once you have the knack. For fillets, put them skin-side down on a chopping board. Use a sharp thin-bladed knife and work in a sawing motion between the skin and flesh, keeping the blade close to the skin which you are pulling taut towards you.

Always check fillets for bones. Tweezers are strong enough to cope with large bones, but make sure they have a really good pinching action to prise out fine ones.

Cooking to perfection

Timing is crucial. Prepare all your other ingredients and cook the fish last. Fish cooks in minutes – just a few minutes more can result in overcooking, especially with small pieces. Fish can be cooked by poaching or simmering in stock (but not boiling), steaming, shallow or deep-frying (if it is coated in batter), grilling, barbecuing, roasting or baking.

Fish can also be microwaved – it's a very quick method, so retains flavour, nutrients and juices, and keeps the skin intact. You need to add very little liquid, but watch the timing. This will vary depending on the thickness and quantity, but 450g/1lb fillets will cook in about 4 minutes. Always slightly undercook it, because 2 minutes of standing time will finish it off perfectly, or you can always pop it back in the microwave for a few seconds more.

Raw fish is translucent, but changes to a more solid white when cooked. Take a closer look by pushing the point of a sharp knife into the fillet and gently parting it in the centre. Whichever method you use for cooking, it is best to stop it when the fish is still slightly translucent; this means it will retain the juices. A few minutes more and it could turn tough and dry. For a whole fish, check the gills. If they have turned from pink to a grey brown, the fish is cooked.

Banish fishy odours

Washing your hands with soap and water doesn't always get rid of the fishy smell. After washing, rubbing your hands with the cut side of a lemon then rinsing works well.

Italian cod and garlic tomatoes

The fish can be stuffed and wrapped up to 1 hour ahead, then chilled.

PREPARATION 15 MINUTES
COOKING 40 MINUTES
SERVES 6

2 unpeeled garlic cloves
3 tbsp olive oil
100g/4oz black olives
900g/2lb tomatoes
2 medium red chillies, deseeded and
   roughly chopped
3 tbsp pesto sauce
2 skinless cod fillets, each about
   450g/1lb
finely grated zest of 1 small lemon
12 slices of prosciutto

Fish lovers can also tuck into a roast. Choose a plump, firm-fleshed fish, such as cod or monkfish. The prosciutto provides contrast in flavour and colour. As this is a very special roast, use succulent unpitted Kalamata olives, fresh pesto (bought or home-made), and good-flavoured, bright red plum tomatoes or ones on the vine.

1 Preheat the oven to 200C/400F/Gas 6. Put the garlic in a roasting tin with 2 tablespoons of oil and roast for 15 minutes, then remove from the oven. Add the olives, tomatoes and chillies and stir. Season well.
2 Spread pesto on one side of a fillet, sprinkle over the lemon zest and season. Lay the other fillet on top, then wrap ham loosely around the fish, tucking in the edges. Season and drizzle over the remaining oil.
3 Put the cod on a rack over the roasting tin. Roast for 20 minutes until the fish is cooked and the tomatoes are starting to break up.
4 Transfer the cod to a plate. Mash the garlic into the pan juices, discarding the skins, and season. Slice the cod and serve with the olives, tomatoes and pan juices.

A full-bodied white Chardonnay is the best choice for this strong-flavoured dish. Choose a European Chardonnay, as this will generally have less fruit and balancing acidity.

Cod and prawn pie

PREPARATION 30 MINUTES
COOKING ABOUT 1 HOUR
SERVES 6

700g/1lb 9oz floury potatoes, sliced
50g/2oz butter, plus more for the
  casserole
1 tbsp olive oil
2 small fennel bulbs, sliced
1 small onion, finely chopped
2 garlic cloves, finely chopped
2 tbsp plain flour
300ml/½ pint milk
150ml/¼ pint dry white wine
142ml/¼ pint carton of single cream
900g/2lb cod, skinned and cut into
  chunks
200g/7oz cooked peeled prawns
3 hard-boiled eggs, shelled and
  quartered
2 tbsp capers, roughly chopped
150g/5oz Gruyère cheese, grated
6 tbsp chopped fresh dill
4 tomatoes, skinned and each cut
  into 8 wedges

Don't be put off by the long list of ingredients. This pie tastes delicious and can be prepared earlier in the day and cooked in the oven when you're ready.

1 Preheat the oven to 200C/400F/Gas 6. Parboil the sliced potatoes for 5 minutes.
2 Heat half the butter with the oil and fry the fennel for 6–7 minutes. Lift out, leaving the butter behind, and stir in the rest of the butter. Add the onion and garlic and cook for 5 minutes.
3 Add the flour and cook, stirring, for 1 minute. Remove from the heat and stir in the milk and wine. Bring to the boil, whisking, and simmer for 2 minutes until thick. Allow to cool, then stir in the cream. Set aside.
4 Butter a 3 litre/5¼ pint casserole and layer half the potato slices in the bottom. Mix together the cod, prawns, eggs, capers, most of the cheese, half the dill and salt and pepper to taste. Spoon the mixture over the potatoes. Layer the remaining potatoes on top, pour over the sauce, then scatter over the fennel and tomatoes. Sprinkle with the remaining cheese and bake for 35 minutes until golden.
5 Sprinkle with the rest of the dill and serve hot.

A chilled top-quality dry cider would make a great match for this new spin on a family favourite; or choose a vin de pays white blend from southern France.

Roast sea bass with Romesco sauce

Make the sauce a day in advance and chill. Remove from the fridge 30 minutes before serving – it should be served at room temperature.

PREPARATION 20 MINUTES
COOKING 1 HOUR 20 MINUTES
SERVES 6

1kg/2lb 3oz baby new potatoes
sea salt
4 tbsp extra-virgin olive oil
2 whole sea bass, each about 1kg/
　2lb 3oz, cleaned and scaled
a few chopped fresh herbs, to garnish
green salad, to serve

FOR THE ROMESCO SAUCE
400g/14oz large ripe tomatoes
6 garlic cloves in their skins
25g/1oz skinned hazelnuts
25g/1oz close-textured white bread
　(with crust removed)
4 tbsp extra-virgin olive oil
1 tsp dried chilli flakes
2 tsp sherry vinegar
1 tbsp tomato purée

Romesco is a famous fish sauce from the province of Tarragona in Spain, where the small hot Romesco peppers are harvested. We use dried chilli flakes, which may not be completely authentic but still make a great-tasting fiery sauce. You may need to order the bass in advance as these fish soon get snapped up (they are in season in the UK from August to March). Make it easier on yourself – get the fishmonger to gut and scale them for you.

1 Preheat the oven to 200C/400F/Gas 6. Make the sauce: put the tomatoes and garlic in a roasting tin and roast for 15 minutes, then add the hazelnuts and bread, drizzled with 1 tablespoon of the oil. Cook for 15 minutes more until the tomatoes and garlic are softened and the nuts are golden. Leave to cool, then remove and discard the skins from the tomatoes and garlic.
2 Spoon the whole lot into a blender, scraping up all the roasting juices. Add the dried chilli flakes, vinegar, tomato purée and plenty of salt and pepper, then process until smooth, adding a splash of water if needed. With the motor still running, drizzle in the remaining oil to make a thick sauce.
3 Tip the potatoes into a large roasting tin. Sprinkle with sea salt, drizzle with 2 tablespoons of olive oil and mix well to coat. Roast for 25 minutes until they are beginning to brown.
4 Rub the remaining oil all over the fish and season well with salt and pepper. Slash the fish diagonally several times on each side. Give the potatoes a good stir in the tin, then lay the fish on top. Roast for 30–45 minutes until the fish is cooked through.
5 Sprinkle with herbs and serve with the potatoes, Romesco sauce and a green salad.

With its spiciness, Romesco sauce is hard to match to wine. Go for a wine from the region, such as Torres Viña Esmerelda.

FISH & SEAFOOD MAIN COURSES • 59

Monkfish and prosciutto kebabs

This is a fragrant alternative to the traditional kebab. Monkfish is a lovely plump fish but a bit pricey, so you could use another firm-fleshed fish, such as huss or cod.

Prepare the kebabs, cover and chill no more than 2 hours before cooking.

PREPARATION 20 MINUTES, PLUS
  20 MINUTES' MARINATING
COOKING 10 MINUTES
SERVES 4 (EASILY DOUBLED)

4 lemons
4 tbsp olive oil
2 tbsp roughly chopped fresh dill
900g/2lb monkfish tails, cut into 24
  chunks (about 4cm/1¼in)
12 slices of prosciutto, each cut into 2
  strips lengthwise
asparagus and rice, to serve

FOR THE DILL SAUCE
5 tbsp dry white wine
2 shallots, finely chopped
175g/6oz butter, chilled and diced
2 tbsp finely chopped fresh dill
squeeze of lemon juice

1 Mix the pared rind of 1 lemon with the oil and dill in a non-metallic dish, then season. Toss in the monkfish chunks to coat. Leave for 20–40 minutes.
2 Preheat a very hot grill or the barbecue until the coals are ashen white. Cut each of the remaining 3 lemons into 6 wedges. Wrap a strip of prosciutto around each piece of fish. Thread them on to 8 skewers, alternating with lemon wedges; you should have 3 wrapped fish pieces and 2 lemon wedges on each. Brush the prosciutto with the marinade. Grill or barbecue the kebabs for 5–7 minutes, turning occasionally.

3 Make the dill sauce: in a pan, simmer the wine and shallots until reduced to about 2 tablespoons. Over a very low heat, gradually whisk in the butter a piece at a time, but don't let it boil. When all the butter has blended in (the sauce should be thickened and glossy), remove from the heat, season and stir in the dill and a squeeze of lemon juice.
4 Serve the kebabs with the dill sauce, rice and asparagus.

Monkfish matches reds as well as whites, so take a cue from the prosciutto's Italian origins and choose a fruity Italian red, such as Valpolicella or Bardolino.

Monkfish au vin

Some people balk at drinking red wine with fish, let alone cooking the fish in it, but it works with monkfish because it has a good firm flesh and lots of character.

Make the sauce (in step 2) up to a day ahead, then reheat and add the fish.

PREPARATION 25 MINUTES

COOKING 20 MINUTES

SERVES 4

900g/2lb monkfish

25g/1oz butter

1 tbsp olive oil

12 shallots, halved if large

225g/8oz chestnut mushrooms, halved

3 small garlic cloves, chopped

sprig of thyme

2 sprigs of parsley

1 bay leaf

2 tbsp brandy

1 bottle of good red wine

2 tbsp redcurrant jelly

2 tbsp plain flour

150g/5oz unsmoked bacon, cut into strips

3–4 tbsp vegetable oil

8 thin slices of French bread

chopped fresh parsley, to garnish

1 Remove the skin and central bone from the fish, then cut it into 4cm/1 1/2in chunks. Season and set aside.

2 Heat the butter and oil in a pan. Sweat the shallots slowly until just brown. Add the mushrooms and brown for a few minutes, then add the garlic, herbs and seasoning. Turn up the heat, add the brandy and carefully ignite. When the flames die down, pour in the wine. Bring to the boil and reduce by half. Stir in the redcurrant jelly and boil for 1 minute.

3 Toss the fish cubes in the flour and add to the sauce. Simmer for 6–7 minutes until tender. Season.

4 Fry the bacon in a tablespoon of the oil until crisp. Remove and drain. Add the rest of the oil and fry the bread to make croûtons.

5 Spoon the fish and sauce on to plates, sprinkle with bacon and parsley and serve with the croûtons.

Choose a light-bodied red wine, such as a Beaujolais-villages. It will be richer and riper than a standard Beaujolais.

Griddled tuna with herbed vegetables

This is the perfect taste of summer. Don't cook the tuna for longer than a minute on each side or it will be dense and hard, not melt-in-the-mouth and succulent.Tuna must be really fresh, so order it a few days before to be sure the steaks are all the same size and really fresh when you pick them up.

Make the herb butter up to 1 day ahead.

PREPARATION 20 MINUTES
COOKING 15 MINUTES
SERVES 6

4 tbsp olive oil, plus more for brushing
250g/9oz cooked new potatoes
2 garlic cloves, finely chopped
250g/9oz green beans
250g/9oz sugar snap peas
250g/9oz cherry tomatoes
6 thick tuna loin steaks, each about
    200g/7oz
6 tbsp chopped mixed chives, parsley
    and dill

FOR THE HERB BUTTER
100g/4oz butter, softened
grated zest and juice of 1 lemon
3 tbsp mixed chopped chives, parsley
    and dill

1 First make the herb butter: mix the butter, lemon zest, half the lemon juice and all the herbs. Season. Spoon on to plastic film, roll up into a sausage shape and chill until needed.
2 Heat the oil in a wok, then fry the potatoes for 1 minute. Add the garlic, beans, sugar snaps and tomatoes and cook for 10 minutes, stirring occasionally, until the vegetables are tender.
3 Meanwhile, heat a griddle pan until hot. Brush the tuna with oil and season, then fry in batches for 1 minute on each side. Transfer to plates and squeeze over a little of the remaining lemon juice.
4 Add the herbs to the hot vegetables and spoon on to warm plates. Put a tuna steak on top. Slice the butter into 12 discs and arrange 2 on each tuna steak.

A fresh, light dish such as this, with its echoes of salade Niçoise, calls for a chilled Sauvignon Blanc or Muscadet-sur-lie.

Pan-fried tuna steaks with baba ghanoush

Make the baba ghanoush earlier in the day, cover and leave at room temperature.

PREPARATION 20 MINUTES
COOKING 30 MINUTES
SERVES 6

6 tbsp olive oil
grated zest of 1 lemon
2 tbsp chopped fresh coriander
6 thick tuna loin steaks, each about 200g/7oz
250g/9oz cherry tomatoes, halved
buttered spinach, to serve

FOR THE BABA GHANOUSH
3 large aubergines, about 900g/2lb in total
3 garlic cloves, roughly chopped
4 tbsp tahini paste
juice of 1 large lemon
1 tsp ground cumin
handful of fresh coriander

Grilled tuna – or another robust-flavoured fish, like swordfish or red mullet – sits well on baba ghanoush, a Middle Eastern aubergine dip flavoured with tahini.

1 First make the baba ghanoush: preheat the grill to high. Grill the aubergines whole, turning them now and then, for 20–25 minutes until blackened. When cool, trim off the stalks, cut the aubergines in half and scoop the flesh into a food processor. Add the garlic, tahini, lemon juice, cumin and coriander. Season, and process until smooth.
2 Mix the oil, lemon zest and coriander. Lightly brush some of the mixture over the tuna and season. Heat 1 tablespoon of the oil in a large frying pan and fry the tuna in batches for 1 minute on each side (just long enough to sear the outsides and keep the fish juicy and tender). Remove from the pan and keep warm. Add the rest of the flavoured oil to the pan, then fry the tomatoes for 1 minute.
3 Divide the baba ghanoush between 6 plates. Arrange a tuna steak and the tomatoes on top. Drizzle over any pan juices and serve with buttered spinach.

Choose a big bold Australian Chardonnay, with ripe fruit and some ageing in oak for extra body; or pick a Retsina for the full Mediterranean effect.

Pan-fried salmon with Pernod sauce

Grilled peppers bring colour and flavour to the sauce and go well with
the Pernod. Lemon juice is a natural partner to salmon and cuts
through the buttery sauce.

PREPARATION 20 MINUTES
COOKING 30 MINUTES
SERVES 6

6 red peppers, quartered and
  deseeded
50g/2oz cold butter
4 shallots, finely chopped
5 tbsp Pernod
1 bay leaf
450ml/³/₄ pint vegetable stock
900g/2lb salmon fillet, skinned
a few drops of oil
squeeze of lemon juice

TO SERVE
steamed new potatoes
lime and lemon wedges

1 Grill the peppers, skin side up, for 15 minutes until the skins are
charred. Allow to cool, then remove and discard the skins. Tear the
peppers into large pieces.
2 Heat half the butter in a large pan and cook the shallots and peppers
for 5 minutes until soft. Add the Pernod and allow to bubble until most
of the liquid has evaporated. Add the bay leaf and stock, bring to the boil
and cook for 20 minutes until reduced by half; remove the bay leaf.
3 Meanwhile, cut the salmon at an angle into 6 thick pieces. Heat a
large frying pan, add a drop of oil and cook the salmon in batches
for 2 minutes on each side. Transfer to a plate and season with salt,
pepper and lemon juice.
4 Using a slotted spoon, remove the peppers from the sauce and divide
between 6 warmed serving plates.
Top with a slice of salmon.
5 Bring the remaining sauce to a
simmer. Cut the rest of the butter
into pieces, then whisk into the
sauce a little at a time, until thick
and glossy. Pour over the salmon
and serve with new potatoes and
lemon and lime wedges.

As aniseed has a dominant flavour, it is best not
to fight it but to complement it with a fairly
restrained Bordeaux Blanc.

Salmon and watercress puff

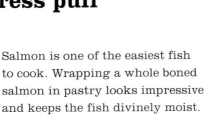

PREPARATION 15 MINUTES, PLUS
 30 MINUTES' CHILLING
COOKING 45 MINUTES
SERVES 6

1.3kg/3lb salmon as 2 matching fillets,
 skinned
bunch of fresh watercress
200g/7oz full-fat soft cheese, softened
grated zest of 1 orange
500g/1lb 2 oz packet of puff pastry,
 defrosted if frozen
beaten egg, to glaze
new potatoes, to serve

FOR THE SALAD
3 oranges, peeled and segmented
bunch of fresh watercress
½ tbsp orange juice
1 tsp balsamic vinegar
1½ tbsp olive oil

Salmon is one of the easiest fish
to cook. Wrapping a whole boned
salmon in pastry looks impressive
and keeps the fish divinely moist.

1 Sprinkle the salmon all over with salt and pepper. Make the filling:
finely chop the watercress and beat it into the cheese with the orange
zest; season. Lay a fillet, skinned-side down, and spread with filling.
Cover with the other fillet, skinned-side up.
2 Roll out half the pastry so it is 2.5cm/1in larger all round than the
fish. Put on a dampened baking sheet; lay the salmon in the centre.
Brush the pastry edges with egg. Roll out the remaining pastry to cover;
trim off excess. Pinch the edges to seal. Brush the top with egg and score
a criss-cross pattern on top. Cover and chill for at least 30 minutes.
3 Preheat the oven to 220C/425F/Gas 7. Bake the puff for 20 minutes,
then glaze again. Lower to 160C/325F/Gas 3 and cook for 20–25 minutes.
4 Make the salad: mix the orange segments and watercress leaves.
Whisk together the orange juice, vinegar and oil with some seasoning.
Toss the salad with this dressing.
5 Serve the puff with the salad and new potatoes.

This party dish definitely deserves a sparkling wine. Match the salmon with a dry sparkling rosé; or
try a crémant, a regional sparkler from France (but not Champagne).

Salmon with horseradish and parsley butter

Make and chill the butter the day
before. Wrap and chill salmon parcels
up to 2 hours ahead.

PREPARATION 10 MINUTES
COOKING 10 MINUTES
SERVES 6

85g/3oz butter, softened
1½ tbsp horseradish sauce
1½ tbsp coarse-grain mustard
1½ tbsp chopped fresh parsley
6 salmon steaks, each about 175g/6oz
2 lemons, thinly sliced
new potato salad with green beans and
 sugar snap peas, to serve

1 Preheat a grill or barbecue to medium-hot (set the barbecue grill
about 10cm/4in above the coals).
2 In a bowl, mix together the butter, horseradish, mustard and
chopped parsley. Form into a sausage shape, wrap in plastic film or
greaseproof paper, then foil. Twist the ends. Chill.
3 Take a very large sheet of foil and cut out 12 circles, 25cm/10in
in diameter (use a double layer of foil for each parcel). Put a salmon
steak in the centre of each double circle and season with salt and
pepper. Lay 3 slices of lemon on each steak and top with a sixth of the
horseradish and parsley butter. Bring the foil up round the fish to
make a loose tent, but seal tightly.
4 Grill or barbecue for 8–10 minutes until the fish is just cooked.
5 Serve with a new potato salad, green beans and sugar snap peas.

A big, bold, well-chilled Australian Chardonnay would make the best match for the flavoured butter
in this dish; or choose a fruity rosé from the south of France or Spain.

Trout and prosciutto with creamy wine sauce

The mild taste of trout fillets goes really well with the slightly smoky flavour of crisp prosciutto. This is a great dinner party dish and can be easily assembled ahead.

Make to the end of step 2 up to
2 hours ahead.

PREPARATION 10 MINUTES
COOKING 25 MINUTES
SERVES 6

knob of butter
12 trout fillets, skinned
6 slices of prosciutto
1 tbsp chopped fresh tarragon
2 tbsp fresh lemon juice
150ml/¼ pint dry white wine
200ml/7fl oz tub of crème fraîche
2 tbsp chopped fresh parsley
saffron or turmeric rice, to serve

1 Preheat the oven to 190C/375F/Gas 5 and butter a large shallow gratin dish.
2 Season the trout fillets on both sides. Cut each prosciutto slice in half lengthwise. Lay a prosciutto strip on a board, put a trout fillet on top, then sprinkle with a little tarragon and lemon juice. Roll up each fillet from the thicker end, then stand it up in the gratin dish.
3 Pour the wine around the rolled fish, then cook, uncovered, for 15–20 minutes until the trout is tender and the prosciutto crisp.
4 Spoon the crème fraîche and parsley around the fish, stirring it in well, then return to the oven for 5 minutes.
5 Serve the fish with the sauce and saffron or turmeric rice.

A delicately flavoured, creamy dish such as this needs a restrained wine with some acidity. Choose an Italian white such as Pinot Grigio.

Smoked haddock and leek risotto

Prepare the haddock and blanch the leeks earlier in the day and keep chilled.

PREPARATION 20 MINUTES
COOKING 25 MINUTES
SERVES 6

900g/2lb smoked haddock
1.7 litres/3 pints vegetable or fish stock
3 large leeks, very thinly sliced
2 tbsp olive oil
25g/1oz butter
500g/1lb 2oz risotto rice
200ml/7fl oz dry white wine
pinch of saffron strands
handful of chopped fresh parsley
handful of snipped fresh chives
25g/1oz Parmesan, freshly grated

Warm and comforting, this dish is perfect for casual entertaining. Make it while you chat to your guests so you can check on the rice and tempt them with the wonderful aromas.

1 Put the haddock, skin-side down, in a shallow pan. Pour over 600ml/1 pint of the stock. Bring to the boil, cover and simmer for 5 minutes until the fish is just cooked. Transfer to a plate to cool.
2 Pour the cooking liquid into a large pan with the rest of the stock and bring to the boil. Add the leeks and cook for 1–2 minutes to soften. Remove and set aside in a bowl. Keep the stock at a simmer.
3 Heat the oil and half the butter in a deep pan. Cook the rice for 5 minutes, stirring, until toasted and translucent. Increase the heat, add the wine and simmer gently. When most of the wine has been absorbed, stir in the stock, reserving about 300ml/$^{1}/_{2}$ pint. Cook over a moderate heat, stirring every few minutes. Add the saffron after 8 minutes. After 15 minutes, taste a grain; it should be creamy with some bite. Add some of the reserved stock if the mixture becomes too dry.
4 Skin the haddock and flake the flesh into chunks. Tip the leeks, fish and any juices into the rice with the herbs, Parmesan and remaining butter. Season to taste. Fold everything into the rice and serve hot.

A crisp Chardonnay would make a lovely match for this dish, possibly even a good Chablis. Alternatively, serve with a chilled Italian beer.

Poultry & game main courses

Poultry is probably among the most popular of choices when it comes to entertaining – it's healthy, it cooks quickly and even the best quality free-range birds are amazingly good value, weight for weight, by comparison with fish and red meat. Fresh chicken breast fillets are a boon to those with impromptu guests or who are forced to shop on the way home. When is poultry cooked? Push a sharp knife into the thickest part of the flesh: if the juices run clear, it's cooked. Duck is often served slightly pink, but make sure ahead of time that all your guests will be happy with this.

Chicken and olive casserole

Make up to 1 day ahead, but don't add the olives, mozzarella or basil. Store in the fridge for up to 1 day. Reheat gently, then add the olives and cheese; or don't add the cheese and freeze for up to 3 months.

PREPARATION 20 MINUTES
COOKING 1¾ HOURS
SERVES 6

1 tbsp olive oil
6 skinless chicken breast fillets,
  each cut into 3–4 pieces
3 red peppers, deseeded and cut
  into chunks
2 onions, chopped
8 slices of smoked back bacon,
  cut into strips
2 garlic cloves, finely chopped
3 tbsp chopped fresh oregano
690g/1½lb jar of passata
50g/2oz pitted black olives
two 150g/5oz mozzarella balls, cubed
fresh basil leaves, shredded
buttered noodles, to serve

Full of Mediterranean flavours, this is perfect for outdoor summer dinner parties. Buffalo mozzarella is best – it's more expensive, but the texture is captivating.

1 Preheat the oven to 180C/350F/Gas 4. Heat the oil in a flameproof casserole. Add the chicken and peppers and brown all over on the hob; remove. Add the onions and bacon; cook for 10 minutes, adding the garlic and oregano for the last minute.
2 Return the chicken and peppers to the casserole with the passata. Cover and cook in the oven for 1 hour. Add the olives, then cook for 30–45 minutes more until the chicken is cooked through and really tender.
3 Remove from the oven and stir in the mozzarella. Season to taste. Sprinkle over the basil and serve with buttered noodles.

An Italian red is the ideal choice with this mixture of ingredients. Choose a relatively light wine that won't fight the flavours of the food, such as a Valpolicella.

Braised chicken with tarragon vegetables

This dish is not suitable for preparing ahead. Make it whenever you can get fresh tarragon.

This classic dish with a thoroughly modern look makes an easy alternative to the Sunday roast.

PREPARATION 20 MINUTES
COOKING 1³⁄₄ HOURS
SERVES 4

1 lemon
1 free-range or corn-fed chicken,
  about 1.6kg/3lb 8oz
25g/1oz butter
1 tbsp olive oil
1 onion, chopped
450g/1lb carrots, chopped
4 celery stalks, chopped
450g/1lb leeks, cut into chunks
1 bay leaf
2 tbsp chopped fresh tarragon
300ml/½ pint chicken stock
150ml/¼ pint dry white wine
4 tbsp crème fraîche
4 tbsp chopped fresh parsley

1 Squeeze the lemon and reserve the juice. Put the lemon halves inside the chicken. Season the chicken inside and out. Heat the butter and oil in a flameproof casserole into which the chicken fits snugly, then fry the chicken all over for about 10 minutes. Remove the chicken.

2 Add the onion, carrots and celery to the pan and fry for 5 minutes. Add the leeks, lemon juice, bay leaf, tarragon, stock, wine and some seasoning. Bring to the boil, then put the chicken on top and reduce the heat to a simmer. Cover tightly and cook gently for 1¹⁄₄–1¹⁄₂ hours.

3 Transfer the chicken to a dish. Remove half the vegetables with a slotted spoon and arrange around the chicken; cover with foil. Remove the bay leaf. In a blender process the remaining vegetables and cooking juices to a smooth purée.

4 Warm the purée in a pan with the crème fraîche and half the parsley, stirring. Season to taste. Sprinkle the remaining parsley over the vegetables on the plate. Serve with the purée.

Cool climate wines are the best choice for such a delicate dish. Try a French white Vin de Pays (use it to cook with too) or a light French red.

Spiced honey-roasted poussin

The tender flesh of the poussin is infused with flavour as the spiced butter melts into it, crisping the skin for a golden finish.

Prepare up to step 2, without glazing with honey or roasting, up to 3 hours ahead and chill.

PREPARATION 20 MINUTES
COOKING 1 HOUR
SERVES 4

2 limes
85g/3oz butter, softened
1 tbsp ground cumin
1 tsp ground turmeric
1/2 tsp hot chilli powder
15g/1/2oz coriander leaves, finely
   chopped
4 poussin, each about 500g/1lb 2oz
2 tbsp clear honey, warmed
1 tsp plain flour
300ml/1/2 pint chicken stock
200g/7fl oz tub of Greek-style yoghurt
mixed basmati and wild rice, to serve
chopped fresh parsley, to garnish

1 Preheat the oven to 200C/400F/Gas 6. Grate the zest from the limes and mix with the butter, cumin, turmeric, chilli and coriander. Season well.
2 Loosen the birds' breast skin. Spread the butter over the flesh and smooth down the skin. Cut each lime into wedges and pop two into each poussin cavity. Put in a roasting tin, brush with honey and roast for about 1 hour, basting occasionally. Transfer the birds to plates; leave in a warm place.
3 Spoon off all but a tablespoon of the fat from the tin and add the flour. Cook for 1 minute, stirring, then add the stock. Bring to the boil, stirring, then bubble gently. Reduce the heat, stir in the yoghurt and warm through gently.
4 Serve the poussins with the gravy and the rice, garnished with parsley.

You don't have to offer wine with a spicy dish like this. A chilled Indian beer makes a good informal match. Alternatively, choose an aromatic dry Riesling from Germany.

ROASTING

Ever since the days when cooks in grand houses cranked up the spit and fixed the meat to the jack for roasting, there has been something majestic about a roast. Today's cooking equipment might be less dramatic, but the roast is still an important part of British culinary life. The experienced family cook might feel able to produce a roast blindfolded, but there is still a great sense of achievement in serving one up – and an equal sense of anticipation from guests.

A roast takes up relatively little of the cook's time and essentially looks after itself (apart from occasional basting). Gravy or sauce can be made from the cooking juices at the last minute.

There's a perfect vegetable for every roast

When choosing which vegetables to serve with your roast, ensure they provide colour that contrasts with the meat or sauce. Traditional choices, such as leeks with lamb or carrots with beef, hold good, but there are endless possibilities. Try to contrast the texture and consistency of vegetables with the meat – for example, serve vegetable purées and spinach with leaner meats, and crisper vegetables with roasts that come with a generous amount of sauce.

Roasting vegetables around a joint allows them to absorb some of the meat's juices. Potatoes or parsnips should come out as crispy as if they were roasted in a separate pan. However, if the recipe includes liquid, such as our Mediterranean leg of lamb on page 89, the consistency will be softer. Tomatoes roasted around fish, such as in our Italian cod and garlic tomatoes on page 56, will soften and release their sweet juices.

Essential equipment

Invest in a top-quality ROASTING TIN – it may cost £30–£40, but should last a life-time. Your tin should be robust and heavy enough not to buckle or distort, no matter how high the temperature in the oven or on the hob. Make sure the tin is not too heavy to hold safely – handles or grips are useful. Choose a size and shape to suit the size of meat or fish you'll roast most often, and if you want a large tin, check it fits your oven. Some are enamelled and others lined with non-stick finish.

Self-basting roasters come with a domed lid, which captures the evaporating steam. Another method, and a helpful way to keep the oven clean when roasting meat, is a roasting bag. Both lidded roasters and bags keep the meat really moist and intensify the flavour. Some tins come with a ROASTING RACK that sits inside, allowing fat to drain as the meat cooks. The alternative is to buy a rack separately to fit your tin. Some are curved to prevent the meat or fish rolling during lifting.

Without a really sharp CARVING KNIFE, meat ends up shredded rather than thinly sliced. A CARVING FORK is also essential to hold the meat steady – if you are inclined to cut yourself, get one with a guard. Most knife blades are now made of stainless steel and don't require constant sharpening.

Choosing the cut

Success in roasting depends largely on choosing the right cut of meat. Tender cuts with a reasonable amount of fat are best; leaner cuts need careful cooking to avoid drying out, or should have fat added in another way, such as wrapping in pastry or bacon.

Good choices are:
Beef – sirloin, topside, top rump, silverside, fillet
Lamb – leg, loin, shoulder, breast, chops (loin or chump)
Pork – loin, shoulder, leg, spare ribs, belly slices, chops (loin, spare rib, chump)
Poultry – whole or spatchcock.

Testing and resting

It's all a matter of taste to what degree people like their roast cooked, but the general rule is that, if you're cooking chicken, turkey and pork, the juices should run clear from the thickest part of the meat. For lamb, beef, venison and duck, the juices can trickle pinky red when you stick in a strong skewer. If in doubt, pop it back in the oven for 10 minutes. It's vital to let your roast rest wrapped in a foil tent before carving. After 10–15 minutes of resting – while you do the vegetables and finish the sauce – the meat juices will have settled, making carving easier and slices more succulent.

Perfect gravy

Once the meat is cooked, remove it from the roasting tin, cover loosely with foil and leave to rest. After pouring off excess fat, the pan juices can be served as they are, or you can deglaze the pan by stirring stock, wine (similar to the one you are serving), Madeira or sherry into the pan on the hob, scraping up all the delicious meaty bits on the base with a wooden spoon. For thin gravy, boil to reduce without thickening. If you add a lot of liquid to the pan juices, add a thickener. Leave about a tablespoon of fat in the pan and whisk in a tablespoon of plain flour, then gradually blend in up to 600ml/1 pint of stock, or a mixture of wine and stock. Keep whisking until it has thickened. If your gravy needs livening up, season it if necessary, then perk it up with redcurrant or cranberry jelly, mustard or a splash of Worcestershire sauce. If adding flour to the fat when making chicken gravy, let it go nut coloured before adding liquid, to improve the colour.

Chicken with wild mushroom cream sauce

Prepare up to the end of step 1 (don't preheat the oven) and chill up to 3 hours ahead.

PREPARATION 20 MINUTES
COOKING 2 HOURS 10 MINUTES
SERVES 6

2.25kg/5lb free-range chicken
knob of softened butter
bouquet garni of fresh tarragon,
  parsley and bay leaves

FOR THE MUSHROOM SAUCE
300g/10oz mixed wild mushrooms,
  sliced or quartered
100ml/3½fl oz Drambuie
450ml/¾ pint fresh chicken stock
142ml/¼ pint carton of double cream
3 tbsp roughly chopped tarragon

Choose a free-range chicken for a better flavour and texture. The Drambuie gives a wonderfully luxurious touch to this delicious sauce.

1 Preheat the oven to 190C/375F/Gas 5. Put the chicken in a roasting tin, rub all over with the butter and season generously. Tie the herbs together with string and put them in the cavity of the bird.
2 Roast the chicken for 2 hours (20 minutes per 450g/1lb, plus an extra 20 minutes). Transfer the roast chicken to a warm plate and loosely cover with foil.
3 Make the sauce: pour off all but a tablespoon of fat from the roasting tin and put on the hob. Fry the mushrooms in this for 1–2 minutes until lightly browned. Keeping the heat quite high, deglaze the pan with the Drambuie for 1–2 minutes, scraping the base of the pan with a wooden spoon. Add the stock and bubble until reduced by half. Stir in the cream and bring just to the boil. Stir in the tarragon and some seasoning.
4 Carve the chicken and serve with the sauce.

The rich, creamy sauce needs a smooth white with enough acidity to balance it. Try a Sauvignon Blanc from the Loire or New Zealand, or a Soave from Veneto in Italy.

Pan-fried chicken with prunes and apricots

PREPARATION 5 MINUTES

COOKING 25 MINUTES

SERVES 6

6 skinless chicken breast fillets,
  each about 150g/5oz

3 tbsp olive oil

2 garlic cloves, chopped

25g/1oz pine nuts

4 tbsp red wine vinegar

300ml/½ pint medium sherry

85g/3oz ready-to-eat dried prunes,
  chopped

85g/3oz ready-to-eat dried apricots,
  chopped

2 tsp light muscovado sugar

cooked couscous, to serve

This sauce is a subtle, intriguing blend of sweet and savoury, and the toasted pine nuts are a perfect contrast with the soft dried fruits.

1 Slash each chicken breast 3 times. Heat the olive oil in a large frying pan, then fry the chicken breasts over a high heat for 2–2½ minutes on each side until golden brown. Sprinkle over the garlic and pine nuts and fry for 1 minute more until the nuts are lightly toasted.

2 Add the red wine vinegar, sherry, chopped prunes and apricots, and sugar to the pan. Bring to the boil and then simmer for 20 minutes, turning once, until the chicken is tender and cooked through.

3 Serve the chicken with the pan juices on a bed of couscous.

Enjoy this on a summer's day with a glass of well-chilled dry fino sherry (sherry isn't just an aperitif); or pick a young white Rioja.

Griddled mango chicken

The chicken can be marinated a day ahead.

PREPARATION 10 MINUTES, PLUS
3 HOURS' MARINATING
COOKING 15 MINUTES
SERVES 6

3 tbsp olive oil

1 tbsp ground coriander seeds

5 tbsp chopped fresh coriander leaves,
plus a handful more for the sauce

3 limes

6 skinless chicken breast fillets, each
about 150g/5oz

2 large ripe mangoes

a little oil, for brushing

200ml/7fl oz carton of coconut cream

1 medium red chilli, deseeded and
finely chopped

Vibrant colours and flavours make this stunning to look at and to eat.

1 Mix the oil with the ground and fresh coriander. Finely grate the zest and squeeze the juice from 1 lime. Mix with the coriander oil. Cut each chicken breast in half horizontally and put in a shallow dish. Rub the oil all over the chicken to coat well and leave to marinate for 3 hours.

2 Heat a griddle pan, then cook the chicken in batches until it is golden on both sides. Remove and keep warm in the oven.

3 Meanwhile, peel and slice each mango into 9 wide slices. Brush lightly with oil. Wipe the griddle, reheat, and griddle the mango for a few minutes, turning, until you get griddle marks and the juices start to run.

4 At the same time, put the coconut cream in a small pan with the juice from a second lime and the chopped chilli. Heat gently for 2–3 minutes until thickened slightly, then stir in the remaining coriander.

5 Cut the remaining lime into wedges. Layer up the chicken slices with the mango slices on each plate. Spoon the coconut chilli sauce around. Serve with a few lime wedges.

This definitely calls for a chilled Thai Singha beer which has some sweetness, and smooths the bite of the chilli.

Spicy chicken with mint raita

PREPARATION 25 MINUTES, PLUS AT
  LEAST 6 HOURS' MARINATING
COOKING 25–30 MINUTES
SERVES 6

1.25kg/2lb 12oz chicken thighs or
  drumsticks, skinned
1 tsp salt
juice of 1 large lemon
300ml/½ pint natural yoghurt
1 small onion, quartered
2 garlic cloves, peeled
2.5cm/1in piece of fresh ginger, peeled
  and chopped
1 tbsp hot chilli powder
1 tbsp paprika
1 tbsp garam masala
naan bread, lemon wedges and mixed
  salad, to serve

FOR THE MINT RAITA
200ml/7fl oz natural yoghurt
2 tbsp chopped fresh mint
½ cucumber, grated

To simulate a tandoor oven, cover the barbecue (if it has a hood) when the coals are very hot, then the chicken will be tender and juicy.

1 Well ahead, ideally the day before, cut 3 slits in each chicken piece and lay in a non-metallic dish. Rub in half the salt and most of the lemon juice. Turn over and repeat with the remaining salt and lemon. Set aside for 20 minutes.
2 Blend the yoghurt, onion, garlic, ginger and spices to a smooth paste in a food processor. Sieve into a clean bowl, then spoon over the chicken and mix well. Cover and chill for 6 hours or overnight.
3 Preheat a hot grill or a barbecue until the coals are white-hot. Remove the chicken from the bowl and shake off the excess marinade. Thread 4 or 5 pieces on to 2 parallel skewers. Cook for 25–30 minutes, turning a few times, until cooked and just blackened.
4 Make the raita by mixing the ingredients and season with salt.
5 Serve the chicken with the raita, naan, lemon wedges and salad.

Cool the spices with an Indian beer such as Kingfisher. If you prefer wine, try a fresh and crisp Sauvignon Blanc from New Zealand or the Loire.

Summer herbed turkey

PREPARATION 10 MINUTES, PLUS AT
  LEAST 2 HOURS' MARINATING
COOKING 10–15 MINUTES
SERVES 6

6 thick-cut turkey breast steaks, each
  about 100g/4oz
lemon and lime wedges, Greek salad
  (tomatoes, cucumber, black olives
  and feta) and pitta, to serve

FOR THE MARINADE
juice and rind of 1 lemon
4 tbsp coarsely chopped fresh parsley
12 fresh mint leaves
12 fresh basil leaves
6 tbsp mild and fruity olive oil

The simple fresh flavours of lemon and herbs are perfect for holiday cooking. These flavours also go well with chicken or fish.

1 Make the marinade: put the lemon rind and juice in a small bowl with the parsley and tear in the mint and basil leaves. Lightly whisk in the oil.
2 Put the turkey in a shallow, non-metallic dish and pour over the marinade. Turn the steaks to coat well, then cover and leave to marinate for 2–4 hours in a cool place.
3 Preheat a hot grill or a barbecue until the coals are ashen white. Oil the grill rack, then remove the turkey from the marinade and put under or directly on the grill; cook for 5–7 minutes on each side, depending on thickness.
4 Season well and serve with lemon and lime wedges, Greek salad and pitta.

Match the Greek salad with one of the 'international-style' whites from Greece, made without a hint of resin; or pick a light fruity red from Languedoc-Roussillon.

Chicken and bean salad with crisp chorizo

This main-course salad has a variety of mild and spicy flavours and crunchy textures. Serve it with bread or a bowl of new potatoes.

To prepare ahead: cook the chicken, allow to cool, take the meat off the bones, blanch the beans, make the dressing.

PREPARATION 20 MINUTES
COOKING 1½ HOURS, PLUS COOLING
SERVES 6 AS A MAIN-COURSE SALAD

1.8kg/4lb chicken
1 lemon
7 tbsp olive oil
175g/6oz green beans, trimmed
 and halved
85g/3oz whole blanched almonds
4 celery stalks, sliced at an angle
1 tsp clear honey
1 tbsp wholegrain mustard
18 thin chorizo slices

1 Preheat the oven to 180C/350F/Gas 4. Put the chicken in a roasting tin. Halve the lemon, squeeze the juice and reserve for the dressing. Put the lemon halves inside the chicken cavity. Season well inside and out and drizzle over 1 tablespoon of oil. Roast for 1¼–1½ hours until the chicken is cooked. Allow to cool and then chill until ready to use.

2 Cook the beans in boiling salted water for 3 minutes; drain and cool quickly under cold water.

3 Put the almonds in a dry frying pan and cook over a medium heat, shaking the pan frequently, until they are evenly browned.

4 Strip the chicken from the bones, tearing it into bite-sized pieces (pic. 1). Mix with the beans, celery and almonds.

5 In a small bowl, whisk 3 tablespoons of lemon juice with the honey and mustard; season. Whisk in the remaining oil until the dressing thickens (pic. 2). Pour over the salad and mix well to coat all the ingredients evenly with dressing.

6 Heat a frying pan, preferably non-stick, and add the chorizo slices in one layer. Fry quickly for about 1 minute, turning once, until crisp and lightly browned (pic. 3). Drain on kitchen paper.

7 Serve the salad in bowls topped with chorizo slices.

Choose a Spanish wine to match the spicy chorizo. If you prefer white, choose a white Rioja; otherwise pick a red from the Navarra region.

Peppered duck with red wine gravy

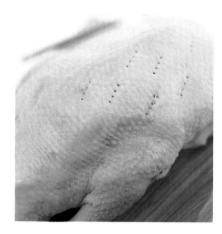

Marinate the fruit up to 2 hours ahead.

PREPARATION 15 MINUTES
COOKING 2 HOURS
SERVES 4

100g/4oz fresh blackcurrants (or
    defrosted frozen)
100g/4oz fresh redcurrants (or
    defrosted frozen)
3 tbsp crème de cassis
1 whole duck, about 2.25–2.75 kg/5–6lb
1 tbsp mixed peppercorns, coarsely
    crushed
1 tbsp plain flour
300ml/½ pint red wine
200ml/7fl oz fresh chicken stock

Marinating the fruit in crème de cassis gives this surprisingly ungreasy duck dish a rich colour and delicious blackcurranty flavour. If you have a spare peppermill (especially a clear acrylic one) it is a good idea to fill it with ready-mixed black, green and red peppercorns for a colourful peppery punch.

1 Put the fruit and cassis in a bowl and leave while you cook the duck.
2 Preheat the oven to 220C/425F/Gas 7. Weigh the duck, then prick the skin all over with a fork; season with peppercorns and salt. Put in a roasting tin.
3 Roast the duck for about 15 minutes until it starts to sizzle. Reduce the heat to 180C/350F/Gas 4 and roast for a further 20 minutes per 450g/1lb. Transfer the duck to a warm plate, cover loosely with foil and leave to rest for 15 minutes.
4 Pour off all but a tablespoon of fat from the tin and place on the hob. Stir in the flour and cook, stirring, until well browned. Add the red wine and stock and cook, stirring, until glossy and thickened slightly. Add the cassis and fruit; simmer gently for 6–8 minutes until the fruit is softened.
5 Carve the duck and serve with the gravy.

A rich red Australian Shiraz makes a bold match for the ripe, spicy sauce. Use the same wine for cooking for the best effect (never skimp on the wine when cooking).

Duck casserole with herbed new potatoes

Make up to the end of step 4 up to a day ahead; allow to cool and chill. Freeze for up to 3 months. Defrost in fridge overnight. Reheat gently, then add the peas and redcurrant jelly.

PREPARATION 15 MINUTES
COOKING 1 HOUR 40 MINUTES
SERVES 4

4 duck legs, each about 300g/10oz
2 tbsp seasoned flour
1 tbsp olive oil
1 large onion, thinly sliced
2 garlic cloves, finely chopped
1 tbsp finely chopped fresh rosemary
300ml/½ pint white wine
300ml/½ pint hot chicken stock
500g/1lb 2oz baby new potatoes,
  halved if large
200g/7oz frozen peas
2 tbsp redcurrant jelly
4 tbsp chopped fresh mint

Redcurrant jelly and mint give a lovely flavour to this non-fatty casserole. Slow cooking means the duck literally falls off the bone when you cut into it.

1 Preheat the oven to 180C/350F/Gas 4. Dust the duck with the seasoned flour. Heat the olive oil in a wide, shallow casserole dish or large roasting tin, then fry the duck legs until well browned all over. Transfer to a plate.
2 Add the onion, garlic and rosemary to the pan and cook for about 5 minutes, stirring frequently, until browned. Drain off any excess fat.
3 Return the duck legs to the casserole or tin, then pour in the wine and bubble rapidly for 5 minutes. Add the stock and potatoes.
4 If using a casserole, cover with a lid; if using a roasting tin, cover with a double thickness of foil, tightly sealed all round. Cook in the oven for 1½ hours.
5 Transfer the dish to the hob. Add the peas and redcurrant jelly and cook for 5 minutes, stirring occasionally, until the jelly has melted. Season with salt and pepper to taste and stir in the chopped mint.

An Alsace wine, with its intensity of flavour, is the ideal choice; look out for a Tokay Pinot Gris, which is rich and aromatic, to match the sweetness of the duck.

Meat main courses

Nothing looks quite so generous and inviting
at the table as a glistening roast joint or a
bubbling casserole. Meat dishes, be they
roasts, braises, casseroles or stews, also lend
themselves well to entertaining, as they
require long, slow cooking, allowing you to
get everything ready well ahead and spend
time with your guests before adding easy
finishing flourishes just before serving. What
could be easier than deglazing a roasting pan
to produce a beautiful glossy sauce in next to
no time? Meats are also the mainstay of today's
new focus of casual entertaining, the barbecue.

Beef in stout with crisp thyme dumplings

Adding chestnuts to this long-standing Irish favourite gives a nutty flavour, and the herb dumplings are cooked uncovered to give them lovely crusty tops.

Make up to the end of step 3 up to 1 day ahead; cool and store in fridge. Reheat before adding the dumplings. Freeze for up to 3 months without the dumplings.

PREPARATION 40 MINUTES
COOKING 2 HOURS 35 MINUTES
SERVES 6

1.25kg/2lb 12oz stewing beef
1 tbsp seasoned plain flour
3 tbsp oil
2 onions, thinly sliced
1 celery stalk, chopped
425ml/³/₄ pint stout
2 tsp light muscovado sugar
1 tbsp tomato purée
1 tbsp Worcestershire sauce
bouquet garni
100g/4oz self-raising flour
2 tsp chopped fresh thyme
2 tsp mustard seeds
50g/2oz butter, frozen in foil
250g/9oz cooked peeled chestnuts

1 Preheat the oven to 160C/325F/Gas 3. Cut the beef into 4cm/1¹/₂in chunks. Put the plain flour in a plastic bag, add the beef and shake well.
2 Heat 2 tablespoons of the oil in a large flameproof casserole, then fry the onions for about 7 minutes; remove. Heat the remaining oil in the dish, then stir-fry the beef over a high heat until sealed all over.
3 Add the onions, celery, stout, 150ml/¹/₄ pint water, the sugar, tomato purée, Worcestershire sauce and bouquet garni. Bring to the boil, scraping up any bits. Season, cover and cook in the oven for 2 hours.
4 About 10 minutes before the 2 hours are up, put the self-raising flour, thyme and mustard seeds in a bowl and season. Grate in the frozen butter and mix well. Gradually mix in 2 or 3 tablespoons of cold water to form a soft dough. Shape into 12 dumplings with damp hands.
5 Stir the chestnuts into the dish; put the dumplings on top. Cook, uncovered, for 20–25 minutes.

The obvious drink with this hearty casserole is stout but, if you find it too rich, choose a full-bodied, rich red, such as a Chilean Cabernet Sauvignon or Cabernet blend.

Chinese tangerine beef casserole

Tangerine peel is a classic Chinese flavouring for braises and other slow-cooked dishes, and is particularly good with beef.

Make up to the end of step 2 up to a day ahead. Chill overnight. Reheat gently, then add the mushrooms and thicken the sauce. Freeze for up to 3 months.

PREPARATION 20 MINUTES
COOKING 2³/₄ HOURS
SERVES 6

4 tangerines or satsumas
1 tbsp vegetable oil
1kg/2lb 4oz piece of topside beef
1 tsp sugar
300ml/¹/₂ pint beef stock
100ml/3¹/₂fl oz soy sauce
100ml/3¹/₂fl oz sherry
1 tbsp grated fresh root ginger
1 onion, sliced
2 star anise
1 tsp Chinese five-spice powder
85g/3oz chestnut mushrooms, sliced
85g/3oz shiitake mushrooms, sliced
2 tsp cornflour
cooked egg noodles, to serve
bunch of spring onions, finely
  shredded, to garnish

1 Preheat the oven to 130C/275F/ Gas 1. Peel the tangerines or satsumas in strips, removing any pith. Put on a baking sheet and bake for 30–45 minutes until crisp and dry but not discoloured. Chop and set aside.

2 Increase the oven setting to 160C/325F/Gas 3. Heat the oil in a flameproof casserole, then fry the beef on all sides to seal. Add the sugar, stock, soy sauce, sherry, ginger, onion, star anise, five-spice powder and tangerine peel. Cover tightly and cook for 1³/₄ hours.

3 Add the mushrooms and cook for 15 minutes more. Transfer the beef to a plate to rest. Meanwhile, mix the cornflour with a little water and stir into the casserole; bring to the boil on the hob, stirring, then simmer until thickened.

4 Slice the beef and serve with the sauce on noodles, garnished with spring onions.

Choose a classic scented and slightly spicy Gewürztraminer from Germany. It's a great way of discovering just how good German wines are.

Pan-fried beef with garlic, rosemary and balsamic vinegar

This classic recipe will impress your guests, yet it's simple to cook. It is also the perfect introduction to the art of deglazing a pan, which produces a beautiful glossy sauce in next to no time.

Bat out the steaks and season up to 2 hours ahead, then chill.

PREPARATION 5 MINUTES

COOKING 15 MINUTES

SERVES 6

6 sirloin steaks, each about 175g/6oz
3 tbsp olive oil
3 garlic cloves, thinly sliced
3 tbsp roughly chopped fresh rosemary
175ml/6fl oz balsamic vinegar
600ml/1 pint beef stock, preferably
  home-made
sautéed potatoes or chips and
  steamed green beans, to serve

1 Put the steaks between two sheets of plastic film and bat out to a 1cm/¹⁄₂in thickness.
2 Heat the olive oil in a large frying pan, then add the garlic and cook until it just begins to sizzle. Remove the garlic with a slotted spoon and allow to drain on kitchen paper.
3 Season the steaks with salt and pepper, then top with a rosemary sprig and transfer to the pan. Cook for 1–2 minutes on each side for medium-rare steak. Increase the cooking time by another minute or two for a more well done steak. (You may have to cook the steaks in batches.) Transfer the steaks and rosemary to a plate and keep warm.
4 Pour the balsamic vinegar into the pan and bubble rapidly, scraping up any bits from the base of the pan, until the mixture has reduced by half. Add the beef stock and allow the mixture to bubble for 4 minutes until reduced and slightly syrupy.
5 Transfer the steaks to warm serving plates and pour over the sauce. Scatter the reserved garlic and rosemary over the top of each steak. Serve with sautéed potatoes or chips and green beans.

The ideal, if extravagant, match is a really good Burgundy, or choose an Italian Bardolino to match the rich Italian balsamic vinegar.

Beef with brandy peppercorn sauce

Keep the shallots in their papery skins while they roast, so they're
extra succulent and give more flavour to the gravy juices.

PREPARATION 10 MINUTES

COOKING 45–55 MINUTES

SERVES 6

2 tbsp olive oil

small knob of butter

1.25kg/2lb 12oz piece of beef fillet

450g/1lb unpeeled shallots

4 tbsp brandy

284ml/½ pint carton of fresh beef stock

4 tsp pickled green peppercorns,
   rinsed and bruised slightly

284ml/½ pint carton of double cream

fresh watercress, to garnish

1 Preheat the oven to 220C/425F/Gas 7. Heat the oil and butter in a
large roasting tin on the hob until very hot. Season the beef, add to
the tin, then cook on all sides to brown. Halve the shallots lengthwise
and add to the tin. Transfer to the oven and roast for 15 minutes.

2 Lower the oven setting to 180C/350F/Gas 4 and cook for 20–30
minutes more, depending on taste. Transfer the beef and shallots to
a plate and cover loosely with foil.

3 Put the tin back on the hob, add the brandy and carefully ignite.
Once the flames have died down, stir in the stock, peppercorns and
cream. Bubble over a medium heat for about 5 minutes until reduced
to a light sauce, then season.

4 Carve the beef and serve with the sauce and shallots. Garnish with
watercress.

Pick a really good mature Burgundy, which will have an enticing blend of fruity and savoury flavours
to complement the meat perfectly.

Rack of lamb with an apricot and mustard crust

Rack of lamb is a very expensive cut, but it's worth it as there is little waste and it looks magnificent. Here this classic dish is given a new twist – a fruity herb crust and stuffing. Ask your butcher to leave the surrounding fat on the lamb so the two racks are joined. This helps to hold the filling in place.

1 Preheat the oven to 220C/425F/Gas 7. Mix together the breadcrumbs, parsley, rosemary, lemon zest, apricots, oil and egg. Spread half the mustard over the inside curves of the lamb, sprinkle with the garlic and season. Spoon half the crumb mixture onto one rack, then press the other rack on top, enclosing the filling and crossing the bones. Tie string around the meat vertically to hold the racks together. Spread the remaining mustard on the outside of the racks and press on the remaining crumb mixture.

2 Put the tied racks in a roasting tin and roast the lamb for 10 minutes, then lower the oven setting to 190C/375F/Gas 5 and cook for a further 50–60 minutes. (If the bone ends begin to burn, cover them with foil.) Transfer the lamb to a serving plate, cover loosely with foil and place the roasting tin on the hob.

3 Make the sauce: add the wine to the roasting tin and bubble rapidly for 3–4 minutes until reduced to a syrup. Add the hot lamb stock, then stir in the mustard and jam to taste. Cook for a few minutes until the jam melts. Whisk in the butter and season to taste.

4 Remove the string from the racks, then slice the lamb into cutlets. Serve with the red wine sauce.

Prepare up to the end of step 2 and chill for up to 3 hours.

PREPARATION 40 MINUTES
COOKING 1¼ HOURS
SERVES 6 WITH LEFTOVERS

150g/5oz fresh white breadcrumbs
4 tbsp chopped fresh parsley
1 tbsp chopped fresh rosemary
1 tsp grated lemon zest
8 ready-to-eat dried apricots, roughly
    chopped
2 tbsp olive oil
1 small egg, beaten
1 tbsp Dijon mustard
2 French-trimmed and chined racks of
    lamb, each with 8 chops, total weight
    about 1.25kg/2lb 12oz
2 garlic cloves, chopped

FOR THE RED WINE SAUCE
300ml/½ pint red wine
300ml/½ pint hot lamb stock
2 tsp Dijon mustard
1–2 tbsp apricot jam
knob of butter, chilled

Serve an old-style Spanish Rioja Reserva – the oak ageing provides wonderful vanilla notes to complement the apricot fruit of the stuffing.

Mediterranean leg of lamb

Prepare up to the end of step 1;
marinate 3–4 hours ahead or overnight.

PREPARATION 15 MINUTES, PLUS
  AT LEAST 1 HOUR'S MARINATING
COOKING 1½ HOURS
SERVES 6

2 tsp coriander seeds
4 tsp fresh oregano, or 1 tsp dried
4 garlic cloves, roughly chopped
150ml/¼ pint white wine
2kg/4½lb leg of lamb
1kg/2¼lb red-skinned potatoes, such
  as Desirée
500g/1lb 2oz large tomatoes
2 aubergines
2 tbsp olive oil
a few fresh oregano sprigs

Here aubergines, potatoes and tomatoes are roasted in and around a leg of lamb, soaking up all the lovely Mediterranean flavours from the wine, garlic and herbs.

For really good results, marinate the lamb overnight in the fridge, then bring to room temperature before cooking.

1 Using a pestle and mortar, crush the coriander, oregano and garlic with some salt and pepper to form a thick paste. Add a splash of wine. Make several slits in the lamb and rub with the spice mixture, then leave for at least 1 hour.
2 Preheat the oven to 220C/425F/Gas 7. Cut the potatoes, tomatoes and aubergines into 1cm/½in thick slices. Put the lamb in a roasting tin, drizzle over the oil and scatter the vegetables around the lamb. Pour over the wine, sprinkle with oregano sprigs, season and roast for 10 minutes. Lower the oven setting to 180C/350F/Gas 4 and roast for 1¼ hours until the lamb is cooked.
3 Transfer the lamb to a plate, cover with foil and allow to rest. If necessary, cook the vegetables for another 10 minutes.
4 Carve the lamb and serve with the vegetables.

Celebrate the sunny flavours of this dish with one of the new wave of young reds from Sicily or Puglia. They're great value, and very bold and direct in style.

Make and shape the burgers earlier in the day or the night before, then chill. Alternatively, pack them between sheets of greaseproof paper and wrap in plastic film or put in a rigid container, and freeze for up to 1 month. Defrost in the fridge overnight.

PREPARATION 15 MINUTES
COOKING 10 MINUTES
SERVES 6

1 onion, roughly chopped
2.5cm/1in piece fresh root ginger, peeled and chopped
2 garlic cloves
bunch of fresh coriander or parsley
2 tsp ground cumin
2 tsp ground coriander
1 tsp ground cinnamon
100g/4oz ready-to-eat apricots, finely chopped
700g/1lb 9oz lean minced lamb
oil, for the grill
6 Middle Eastern-style bread rolls, or other rolls of your choice
8 tbsp mayonnaise
2 tsp harissa paste (see above)
lettuce, tomato and cucumber slices, to serve

Moroccan lamb burgers

If you're going to have burgers on a barbecue, go for home-made every time. These ones are deliciously fruity and spicy. Harissa is a very spicy paste used in North African cooking. Available in most large supermarkets, it is made from chillies and a rich blend of spices, such as coriander, cumin and paprika, all combined in an oil and vinegar paste.

1 Put the onion, ginger, garlic and coriander or parsley in a food processor and process until finely chopped. Add the spices, apricots (pic. 1), lamb and plenty of salt and pepper, then pulse until just mixed – do not overmix as it is best to keep the mixture slightly chunky. Shape into 6 burgers, keeping them separate with squares of greaseproof paper (pic. 2).
2 When the barbecue is hot, put the burgers straight on to the oiled grill and cook for 4–5 minutes on each side.
3 Split and toast the rolls on either or both sides, depending how you like them. Mix together the mayonnaise and harissa. Serve the burgers in the buns with a little lettuce, tomato and cucumber, with the spicy mayonnaise on the side.

Eat Moroccan, drink Moroccan. The country's wines are coming back into fashion; there are plenty of good-quality, good-value bottles around.

THE INFORMAL JOYS OF BARBECUING

You know summer has arrived when you get wafts of those wonderfully aromatic, smoky flavours of fire-roasted food in your garden. A little charring and caramelizing and suddenly commonplace foods prove irresistible. Barbecuing is a great informal way of entertaining, especially on a summer evening.

One of the nicest things about barbecues is that everyone can pitch in, so delegate the sausage turning, kebab basting and salad dressing, and make the most of the informal, relaxed atmosphere.

Essential equipment

Buy a BARBECUE that matches your needs. It's not worth investing in a large expensive model if you only use it once a year. Check out the cooking space on the grill, which can be surprisingly small on barbecues that appear large.

Decide if you want a stand-alone barbecue or a portable tabletop model. Do you want traditional charcoal-fired or gas? Take into account storage space, and buy a weather-proof hood so you can leave it outside if you're short of space. If buying a self-assembly barbecue, check the weight and stability once constructed.

Disposable barbecues are quick and easy to use, and the food still has that lovely smoky flavour. You will need a grill rack if the barbecue does not come with one. Shelves from your oven or grill will do nicely.

You will find TONGS essential for turning the coals in the fire and moving food around the grill. Long-handled tongs are best for all jobs. Check they do actually meet, grab food well, and hold it securely. It's best to colour-code them – a pair for raw food, another for cooked food, and one for moving the coals.

Also consider a FLAT SPATULA for turning fish and burgers or other delicate items, and a long-handled FORK for spearing steaks or larger pieces of meat to turn them over, and for guiding other food round the grill.

HINGED BASKETS are also useful: the fish-shaped ones are great for cooking whole fish; square and rectangular ones for vegetables, seafood and thin cuts of meat that might slip through the gaps in the grill. Baskets also make turning much easier. Oil the basket well before you load in the food to stop it sticking. The food should fit snugly inside, so it stays whole without damage.

Choose sturdy flat or twisted SKEWERS so the food doesn't move around – the longer the better. Double-pronged skewers are even better at holding runaway foods, like sausages. Bamboo and wooden skewers are fine for light, quick-cooking foods like prawns and vegetable kebabs. If you soak the skewers in cold water for about 30 minutes, there's less chance of them charring.

For applying oil and sauces during cooking, a standard PASTRY BRUSH will do the job, but a paintbrush (for food use only, of course) is more efficient for heavy-duty marinades. Keep one brush just for oiling the grill.

OVEN GLOVES are an obvious requirement, but easily forgotten – needed for handling hot items such as the grill shelf.

Start well in advance

Barbecuing is child's play, provided you get the coals lit and to the right temperature exactly when you need to cook. Even though barbecues are an informal way of entertaining, if you light the coals too late, your guests will be hanging around. Gas-fired barbecues are far easier to control, but still need about 10 minutes to heat up before you can start cooking. If you buy a new barbecue, have a test run before inviting friends round or get an expert barbecuer to help you.

How to start the fire

The secret to successful barbecuing is knowing how your fuel burns – fast or slow. You can use wood, but the heat is short-lived, or you could use sticks to start the fire

(try 'flavoured' woods like oak, cherry, hickory and maple, sold in small ready-to-use pieces), then add lumpwood charcoal or briquettes.

Charcoal gets hotter than briquettes, which are small lumps made from compacted coal, sawdust and wood. Some briquettes and lumpwood are impregnated with lighting fuel for instant lighting – all you do is put it straight on the barbecue and light it.

Adding flavour and aroma

Coals and fuel for the fire may be imbued with aroma – you can add woody herbs, such as rosemary, thyme and sage, or use rosemary twigs or lemon grass stems as skewers.

Using marinades

The fierce heat of a barbecue can dry food quickly. Marinating food before cooking absorbs some of the liquid along with the flavourings, and gives a protective layer. Marinating also tenderizes food, so it can be cooked faster. Dry rubs with seasoning, herbs and spice mixtures will also flavour food and give a coating, but will not prevent drying.

Barbecue watch points

Keep food chilled and covered until just before you are ready to cook.

Keep separate tongs and basting brushes for raw and cooked food as they could transfer food poisoning bacteria.

Don't crowd the grill by trying to cook everything at once. Give food space for the heat and smoke to penetrate.

If the heat is too high, you'll char the outside of food, but the inside will still be raw. Check carefully and always make sure food is cooked through (though not overcooked).

Avoid accidents by setting barbecues up on level ground away from strong winds. Don't use petrol, spirit or lighter fuel to ignite the barbecue, keep water to hand, and put out the barbecue when you've finished cooking.

Oriental lamb with mushrooms

PREPARATION 10 MINUTES, PLUS
 20 MINUTES' MARINATING
COOKING 10 MINUTES
SERVES 6

750g/1lb 10oz lean lamb steaks, cut
 into thin strips
6 tbsp dry sherry
6 tbsp dark soy sauce
4 tsp dark sesame oil
1 tbsp cornflour
1 tbsp sesame seeds
1 tbsp vegetable oil
4 garlic cloves, finely chopped
1cm/¹/₂in piece of fresh root ginger,
 finely grated
200g/7oz horse mushrooms, halved
bunch of spring onions, thinly sliced
boiled rice, to serve

Cutting the meat into thin slivers means it absorbs all the Oriental
flavours of the marinade in the time it takes you to prepare the rest
of the meal. Horse mushrooms look a bit like long button mushrooms,
but have a more concentrated flavour with a slight hint of aniseed.
They are available in packs in some supermarkets; if you can't get
them, use open-cup or chestnut mushrooms.

1 Mix together the lamb, sherry, soy, sesame oil and cornflour.
Allow to marinate for 20 minutes.
2 Heat a wok, then dry-fry the sesame seeds until golden brown.
Remove and set aside.
3 Drain the meat, reserving the marinade. Heat the vegetable oil
in the wok, then stir-fry the lamb for 3 minutes until browned.
4 Add the garlic, ginger, mushrooms, half the spring onions and
the marinade, and cook for 2 minutes until the spring onions
start to soften.
5 Sprinkle with the sesame seeds and remaining spring onions,
and serve with rice.

Choose a fine Gewürztraminer for this classic stir-fry, as its aromas are full yet fresh enough
to match this rich dish.

Griddled lamb steaks with apricot salsa

If you thought salsa had to be a tomato-based sauce, think again. This uses spicy harissa paste mixed with nuts and dried fruit. Loose leaves or bags of unwashed spinach need careful sorting, but the leaves are thick, with a robust texture and flavour ideal for this recipe, so it's worth the effort.

Prepare the salsa up to 1 day ahead and chill.

PREPARATION 15 MINUTES
COOKING 10 MINUTES
SERVES 6

500g/1lb 2oz fresh spinach
olive oil, for brushing
6 lamb leg steaks
knob of butter
freshly grated nutmeg

FOR THE SALSA
1 tsp cumin seeds
25g/1oz blanched whole almonds
4 fresh apricots, stoned
grated zest and juice of 1 lemon
½ tsp harissa paste (see page 90)
1 tsp clear honey

1 First make the salsa: toast the cumin seeds and almonds in a dry frying pan. Roughly chop the apricots, then put in a food processor with all the salsa ingredients, and season. Pulse until everything is mixed, but the salsa is still chunky.

2 Put the spinach in a large pan, cover and cook for 5 minutes until wilted.

3 Heat a griddle and brush with oil. Season the lamb, then cook on each side for 1–2 minutes for pink (for best results); longer for more well done according to taste.

4 Meanwhile, drain the spinach thoroughly, squeezing out any excess liquid with the back of a spoon. Return to the pan, stir in butter and season with salt, pepper and nutmeg.

5 Divide between 6 plates, and top with a lamb steak and some salsa.

Choose a full-bodied fruity red, such as a Californian Zinfandel.

Braised lamb à la Grecque

Stuffing is a lovely way to add an intriguing flavour to braised meat. The saltiness of the feta and the fruitiness of the figs combine to make a perfect marriage of flavours with lamb. A butterflied leg of lamb describes its shape after the bone has been removed and the meat is spread out. This makes it easier to carve and provides a cavity for the stuffing. Get your butcher to bone the lamb for you (try to give him some notice), as it is quite hard to do yourself.

The lamb can be stuffed the day before.

PREPARATION 30 MINUTES
COOKING 2½ HOURS
SERVES 6–8

8 ready-to-eat dried figs, chopped
200g/8oz feta, chopped
2 garlic cloves, finely chopped
4 tbsp chopped fresh coriander
2 tbsp chopped fresh mint
2kg/4½lb leg of lamb, boned and butterflied (see above)
12 bay leaves
2 tbsp olive oil
4 red onions, thinly sliced
100ml/3½fl oz balsamic vinegar
300ml/½ pint red wine
2 tbsp clear honey

1 Preheat the oven to 190C/375F/Gas 5. Mix together the figs, feta, garlic and herbs, and season well. Open out the lamb and scatter over the mixture (pic. 1). Fold the lamb back over the stuffing and tie at intervals with string. Slip the bay leaves under the string, then season the lamb.
2 Heat the oil in a large flameproof casserole or roasting tin. Brown the lamb on all sides; remove. Add the onions to the tin, season and cook for 10–15 minutes, stirring. Add the vinegar, wine and honey (pic. 2) and bubble rapidly for 5 minutes, then put the lamb on top.
3 Cover with a tight-fitting lid or double thickness of foil, sealing all round, and cook for 1½ hours, basting twice with the juices. Remove the cover and cook for another 30 minutes until well browned (pic. 3).
4 Transfer the lamb to a plate, cover with foil and rest. If the gravy is a bit thin, bring to the boil and boil rapidly for 2–3 minutes.

The best match for the feta and herbs is a beefy Mediterranean red. Go for an Italian from Puglia; or try one of the new wave European-style Greek reds.

Pork and spicy sausage bean hotpot

The hotpot can be made completely up to a day ahead. Reheat gently before carving. Freeze for up to 3 months.

PREPARATION 20 MINUTES
COOKING 4½ HOURS
SERVES 6

1.3kg/3lb boned and rolled shoulder of pork (with rind on)
1 tbsp olive oil
250g/9oz spicy sausages, such as chorizo, sliced
2 large onions, chopped
2 celery stalks, chopped
1 tsp English mustard powder
2 tbsp black treacle
2 tbsp wine vinegar
4 whole cloves
2 tbsp light muscovado sugar
2 tbsp tomato purée
350g/12oz dried haricot beans, soaked overnight

Here spicy sausages are added to this variation of the traditional American dish, Boston baked beans. Chorizo gives the dish a lovely smoky kick, but you could use a herby sausage like Toulouse.

1 Preheat the oven to 180C/350F/Gas 4. Season the pork (generously if you want a good crackling). Heat the oil in a large casserole with a lid. Add the pork and brown all over; remove. Add the sausages, onions and celery and cook for 10 minutes until the onions start to brown.

2 Stir in the mustard, treacle, vinegar, cloves, sugar and tomato purée. Drain the beans, rinse and stir into the pan. Sit the pork on the beans and pour in enough water to just cover the beans.

3 Cover and cook for 4½ hours until the meat is cooked through, removing the lid for the last hour. Put the meat on a plate, cover with foil and allow to rest for 15 minutes.

4 Carve the pork and serve with the beans.

You could drink a full red wine with this, but why not try a chilled beer? Choose an American beer with a crazy name, such as Pete's Wicked Bohemian Pilsner or Mickey's Big Mouth.

Oriental pork loin with crispy crackling

Subtly spiced with soy sauce and five-spice powder, roast pork and potatoes never tasted so good. Serve with steamed mangetout or stir-fried Chinese cabbage.

Prepare to the end of step 1 several hours ahead.

PREPARATION 20 MINUTES, PLUS
  1 HOUR'S MARINATING
COOKING 2 HOURS
SERVES 6

2kg/4½lb pork loin (with rind on)
coarse sea salt
2 tsp Chinese five-spice powder
3 tbsp soy sauce
12 potatoes, halved
150ml/¼ pint medium-sweet sherry
450ml/¾ pint vegetable stock
1 tbsp cornflour
4 spring onions, sliced at an angle

1 Carefully slice the rind off the pork, leaving as much fat on as possible. Dry the rind with kitchen paper; brush a little olive oil over the outer skin and season well with coarse sea salt. Put the pork in a large dish and sprinkle over the five-spice powder. Cover and chill both the pork and rind for 1 hour.

2 Preheat the oven to 200C/400F/Gas 6. Drizzle the soy sauce over the pork and rub into the flesh. Put the pork in a roasting tin and put the potatoes around it. Cut the rind into 1cm/½in wide strips and put in a separate tin, rind-side up.

3 Roast the pork and rind for 10 minutes, then lower the oven setting to 180C/350F/Gas 4 and cook for 1 hour 50 minutes, basting the pork and turning the potatoes occasionally. Transfer the pork, pork rind and potatoes to a plate and keep warm; allow to rest.

4 Pour off all but a tablespoon of fat from the tin and place on the hob. Bring to the boil and deglaze with the sherry. Add the stock and bring to the boil. Mix a little cold water into the cornflour, then pour this into the roasting tin and stir until the pan juices have thickened slightly. Season, stir in the spring onions and heat through.

5 Carve the pork and rind, and serve with the potatoes and pan juices.

This roast demands a really good wine. The Oriental style needs an aromatic grape variety, and one of the best is Alsace Pinot Gris. It's worth splashing out on a Grand Cru.

Caribbean barbecued jerk ribs

Make the marinade and marinate the ribs the day before.

PREPARATION 15 MINUTES, PLUS AT
  LEAST 2 HOURS' MARINATING
COOKING 20–25 MINUTES
SERVES 6

juice and grated zest of 1 lime
about 5 tbsp white wine or cider
  vinegar
1 onion, roughly chopped
2 Scotch bonnet or red chillies,
  quartered and deseeded
2 garlic cloves, quartered
1/2 tsp ground allspice
1/4 tsp ground cinnamon
50g/2oz fresh root ginger, peeled
  and chopped
handful of fresh thyme sprigs,
  leaves removed, or 1 tsp dried
1/4 tsp ground black pepper
100ml/31/2fl oz soy sauce
2 tbsp dark muscovado sugar
4 tbsp oil
1.8kg/4lb (about 18–20) pork ribs
lime wedges, to serve (optional)
mixed salad and rice cooked with
  herbs, to serve

It's the Scotch bonnet chillies that give this pork its bite, so wear rubber gloves when preparing them, or use milder chillies if you prefer.

1 Make the lime juice up to 100ml/3½fl oz with the vinegar. Put the onion, chillies, garlic, allspice, cinnamon, ginger, thyme leaves and black pepper in a food processor and process until smooth. Add the lime vinegar, soy, lime zest, sugar and oil, and process again.
2 Arrange the ribs in one layer in a non-metallic dish and brush over the mixture. Leave to marinate in the fridge for at least 2 hours.
3 Heat the barbecue coals until ashen white (about 1 hour). Put the grill 15cm/6in above the coals and oil it well. Cook the ribs, flesh-side up, for 5 minutes, then turn and cook for 5 minutes more. Cook for another 10–15 minutes, turning now and then, until tender inside but beginning to char on the edges.
4 Serve the ribs with lime wedges if you like, and a mixed salad and some rice cooked with herbs.

Serve a Caribbean rum punch: blend 1¼ cups rum, 2¼ tablespoons each lime and orange juice and 1½ tablespoons honey. Serve with ice and a dash of angostura bitters.

BRAISING AND CASSEROLING

Braises and casseroles are among the most satisfying of dishes – to eat and to cook – and for entertaining they have many advantages. All the real work can be done in advance, and such dishes are often best made a day ahead, giving flavours time to intermingle and mature.

Braises and casseroles are usually self-contained, making their own sauce during cooking and needing at most a starchy accompaniment (potatoes, bread, rice) and perhaps a green vegetable or salad. Most of the recipes work best in larger quantities – it's hardly worth making a braise or casserole for just two people.

Braising refers to the method of cooking in the oven, while the casserole is the dish in which that cooking takes place, but for modern cooks the two terms tend to overlap. For a braise, meat and at least some of the vegetables are browned first before cooking, to give depth, colour and flavour. This requires a cooking pot that can withstand direct heat as well as the less fierce heat of the oven, and it must be big enough to hold all the ingredients. Heavy metal pots are the most satisfying, but you can brown individual elements in a frying pan, then bring them together in a pottery casserole for the oven. (You'll need a tight-fitting lid to stop evaporation, or cover the dish with foil and tuck over the edges to seal.)

A braise is a refined dish because it allows for layers of flavour to build within the pot. Ingredients such as herbs, olives or redcurrant jelly are often added in the latter stages to add fresh flavour.

Essential equipment

The best CASSEROLES are those that conduct heat well and distribute it evenly. They should also have a tight-fitting lid to seal in moisture and flavour, and to stop the meat drying out. Quality enamelled cast iron pans can last a lifetime and are well known for their durability. Like their stainless steel equivalent, their heavy flat bases are ideal for use on the hob for browning meat and

sautéing vegetables for a braised dish, and in some recipes for deglazing to make a sauce afterwards. A shallow casserole, or buffet or serving casserole, is ideal for the table.

A TAGINE is a glazed earthenware dish with a shallow base and a conical lid that collects steam and bastes the stew of vegetables, fish, chicken or meat. Often this slow cooked stew is in a sweet spicy sauce and served with couscous. Sometimes the food is cooked without the lid to give a crusty finish.

The secret of thickening casseroles

A good casserole recipe contains the right amount of liquid to thicken meat juices, stock and vegetables naturally into a perfect sauce. For a thicker sauce, dust the meat with seasoned plain flour before sautéing or browning. Or whisk a butter and flour paste (beurre manié) into the casserole towards the end of cooking. Mash 25g/1oz each of flour and softened butter to a paste, then whisk into the liquid bit by bit.

A trick that many chefs are using is to put a large whole peeled potato in at the start of the oven baking of a slow-cooked casserole. This is fished out at the end, liquidized with some of the cooking juices and used as a thickener – you can add as much or little as you need, and it's lighter than a beurre manié.

Make the most of your ingredients

There's no need to use premium cuts as braising and casseroling make tougher, less expensive cuts of meat meltingly tender. The juices from the meat pass into the sauce to create a complex flavour. Allow about 140g–175g/ 5–6oz meat (off the bone) per person.
Beef – Use chuck, blade or stewing steaks, skirt, flank, topside, leg (knuckle and shank) or shin.
Lamb – Use middle, neck or scrag end of neck, best end of neck chops, or leg.
Pork – Use shoulder, spare rib, hand and spring, pigs' trotters.

Fish – Use firm-fleshed fish, such as monkfish or cod. Add shellfish towards the end of the cooking to add flavour without overcooking it.
Vegetables – Celery, fennel and chicory are among the most commonly braised vegetables. Their stringy texture is softened and they don't disintegrate into a pulp. Onions and carrots are also good. Red cabbage is another seasonal braise candidate.
Game – Birds such as pheasant, grouse, partridge and pigeon are usually cooked whole because they are small. Only the youngest game birds are suitable for roasting, so that leaves plenty of scope for enjoying braised and casseroled game.

Marinating and flambéing

Marinating meat in alcohol and/or spices before braising improves the intensity of the flavour of the meat and the sauce, and also helps tenderize the meat.

Flambéing is a technique that adds a greater depth of flavour to stews and braises. Only strong spirits, such as brandy or whisky, are really successful as you need a high alcohol content to flambé. When making a casserole, the meat is usually flambéed after its initial browning and before the other ingredients are added. Stand well back and use a long taper if you have one.

What can go wrong

UNDERCOOKED Temperature too low or the cooking time too short. Continue to cook and/or raise the temperature.
DRY Caused by overcooking, too high a temperature or wrong cut of meat.
TOUGH Poor-quality meat, old game or lack of fat in the meat.
LACK OF FLAVOUR Check seasoning first; if there is enough salt and pepper, add one of the following (whichever suits the basic flavour) at the end of cooking: mustard, pesto, Worcestershire sauce, Tabasco or other hot pepper sauce.

Venison with herbed pumpkin wedges

Venison makes a lovely change from beef for a Sunday roast and made this way it is full of rich flavours. Roast the pumpkin with it and serve with some roast potatoes.

Prepare to end of step 1 (don't preheat the oven) up to 4 hours ahead; chill.

PREPARATION 20 MINUTES
COOKING 40 MINUTES
SERVES 6

1.5kg/3lb 5oz piece of venison fillet
3 tbsp olive oil
1.3kg/3lb unpeeled pumpkin
4 bay leaves
5 fresh thyme sprigs
4 shallots, finely chopped
2 garlic cloves, finely chopped
1 tbsp crushed juniper berries
grated zest and juice of 1 orange
150ml/¼ pint port
600ml/1 pint lamb or beef stock
1 tbsp redcurrant jelly
knob of cold butter

1 Preheat the oven to 220C/425F/Gas 7. Tie the venison with string at 5cm/2in intervals; season.
2 Heat a tablespoon of oil in a roasting tin, then fry the meat all over to seal. Cut the pumpkin into wedges, add to the roasting tin and season. Add 3 bay leaves, 3 thyme sprigs and the remaining oil. Turn the pumpkin wedges in the oil and roast for 30–35 minutes, turning the wedges twice, until the meat is slightly pink inside. Put the meat and pumpkin on a plate and cover with foil.
3 Drain all but a tablespoon of oil from the tin, then add the shallots and garlic. Cook for 5–7 minutes, until the shallots start to go golden brown. Add the juniper berries and the orange zest and juice, and bubble for 30 seconds. Add the port and remaining bay and thyme, then cook for 5 minutes more, stirring occasionally, until reduced by half.
4 Stir in the stock and boil until reduced by half. Sieve into a clean pan, rubbing gently with the back of a spoon. Return to the heat, add the jelly and stir to melt. Whisk in the butter until thickened and glossy; season.
5 Carve the meat and serve with the sauce and the pumpkin.

This powerful dish is great with the classic Italian reds bursting with fruit and flavour. Choose a mature Barolo or Barbaresco which has had time to age and soften.

Vegetables & salads

Vegetables are supremely versatile – take potatoes: they can be served as a plate of creamy, buttery mash, a crispy roast or the best-ever French fry. Vegetables can enliven and enrich a meal with taste, texture and colour – think of rich red cabbage, roasted parsnips and crunchy green beans. Low in fat and essential for good health, vegetables are no longer seen as mere accompaniments – fresh salads are a tasty meal in themselves, and are quick to prepare for a simple supper with friends.

Moroccan-style vegetable tagine

Make the tagine the day before and reheat just before serving.

PREPARATION 30 MINUTES

COOKING 40 MINUTES

SERVES 6

2 tbsp olive oil

2 onions, chopped

2 garlic cloves, finely chopped

500g/1lb 2oz butternut squash or
  pumpkin, cut into batons

2 large carrots, cut into batons

500g/1lb 2oz potatoes, cut into batons

1 tsp ground cumin

1 tsp ground ginger

1 tsp ground cinnamon

6 tomatoes, roughly diced

250g/9oz broad beans

400g/14oz can of chickpeas, drained

1.2 litres/2 pints hot vegetable stock

pinch of saffron strands

4 tbsp chopped fresh parsley

juice of 1 lemon

2–3 tsp harissa paste (see page 90)

FOR THE HONEY COUSCOUS

2 tbsp clear honey

850ml/1 1/2 pints boiling water

450g/1lb couscous

85g/3oz pine nuts

85g/3oz seedless raisins

2 tbsp olive oil

This colourful blend of vegetables scented with saffron, lemon and parsley works beautifully served with a honey-sweet couscous.

1 Heat the oil in a large pan and cook the onions, garlic, squash, carrots, potatoes and spices for 10 minutes, stirring often.

2 Stir in the tomatoes and cook for 2 minutes, then add the beans, chickpeas, stock and saffron. Bring to the boil, then reduce the heat and simmer for 30 minutes.

3 Meanwhile, make the honey couscous: mix the honey and a pinch of salt into the boiling water. Pour this over the couscous in a heatproof bowl. Stir in the pine nuts and raisins. After 15 minutes, stir in the olive oil and fluff up with a fork.

4 When the stew has simmered for 30 minutes, stir the parsley and lemon juice into it and season.

5 Transfer about 150ml/1/4 pint of the cooking liquid to a jug and stir in the harissa. Serve the stew with the harissa sauce and the honey couscous.

Try to find a big, bold Moroccan red; alternatively, try an Algerian Sidi Brahim, or a New World wine, such as an Argentinian Malbec.

Roasted roots with Indian spices

To prepare ahead: up to 1 hour in advance, grind the spices and mix with the oil and butter (do not chill). Peel and chop the vegetables, seal in a polythene bag and chill.

PREPARATION 10 MINUTES
COOKING 1 HOUR
SERVES 6

2 tsp cumin seeds
2 tsp coriander seeds
2 tsp mixed peppercorns
1 tsp dried crushed chillies
3 tbsp olive oil
25g/1oz butter, melted
700g/1lb 9oz floury potatoes,
 such as Maris Piper or Cara
450g/1lb carrots
450g/1lb parsnips
sea salt flakes

This is a great dish for enlivening a roast chicken or leg of lamb, or it can be served as an accompaniment to a spicy main course. Grinding your own spices really brings out their flavour. To give your vegetables a lovely crisp roasted finish, add salt after cooking rather than before – if you sprinkle it over vegetables before roasting, the salt draws out their moisture, which means they'll steam rather than roast.

1 Preheat the oven to 200C/400F/Gas 6. Using a pestle and mortar, pound the cumin, coriander, peppercorns and chillies until they are coarsely ground (pic. 1). If you don't have a pestle and mortar, put the spices in a cup or bowl and grind with the end of a rolling pin. Mix the ground spices with the oil and butter.
2 Cut the potatoes, carrots and parsnips into chunks or halve them lengthwise. Put in a roasting tin large enough to take them in a single layer. Pour the spice mixture over the vegetables and toss everything together so the vegetables are well coated (pic. 2).
3 Roast for about 1 hour until the vegetables are golden and crisp, turning them a couple of times during cooking so they brown evenly. Sprinkle with sea salt and serve.

Green beans with crispy Parma ham

To prepare ahead: trim and blanch the beans, cool in ice-cold water, then dry and chill.

PREPARATION 15 MINUTES
COOKING 5 MINUTES
SERVES 6

450g/1lb green beans, trimmed
1 tbsp olive oil
85g/3oz Parma ham or prosciutto, torn into strips
1 bunch of spring onions, sliced at an angle
1 tbsp balsamic vinegar

Parma ham fries to a crisp very quickly and the salty flavour goes well with most green vegetables. This treatment also works very well with leeks or spinach.

1 Bring a pan of water to the boil, add some salt and blanch the beans for 3–4 minutes.
2 Meanwhile, heat the oil in a large frying pan or wok and fry the ham until crisp. Add the spring onions and the vinegar and stir for 1 minute.
3 Drain the beans and tip them into the pan. Toss to coat the beans in oil. Season to taste with salt and pepper and serve immediately, while they are still hot.

Peas with young garlic and spring onions

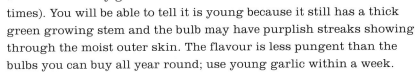

Pod the peas and slice the onions up to 2 hours in advance; cover with plastic film.

PREPARATION 10 MINUTES
COOKING 8 MINUTES
SERVES 6

1 fresh young garlic bulb
1 bunch of spring onions, trimmed
25g/1oz butter
1 tbsp olive oil
450g/1lb fresh podded or frozen peas
(if you buy peas in their pods, get at least twice the weight you need to allow for the weight of the pods)

Don't be put off by the whole bulb of garlic in the ingredients. Cooked garlic is far less pungent than raw, so the flavour is not overpowering. Young garlic is harvested in late spring, so look for it in the shops from mid-June until July (use half a bulb of ordinary garlic at other times). You will be able to tell it is young because it still has a thick green growing stem and the bulb may have purplish streaks showing through the moist outer skin. The flavour is less pungent than the bulbs you can buy all year round; use young garlic within a week.

1 Separate the cloves of garlic and peel them. Cut each clove lengthwise into 4–5 slices. Slice the spring onions.
2 Heat the butter and oil in a pan and gently fry the garlic and onions until softened, about 2 minutes. Stir in the peas, coating them well in the juices. Then cook gently, stirring occasionally, for 3 minutes for frozen peas or 5 minutes for fresh.

Steamed vegetables with lemon tarragon butter

To prepare ahead: peel and cut the vegetables; cover with plastic film.

PREPARATION 10 MINUTES
COOKING 10 MINUTES
SERVES 6

900g/2lb mixed vegetables, such as baby carrots, baby courgettes and sugar snap peas
175g/6oz butter, cut into cubes
2 shallots, finely chopped
5 tbsp tarragon vinegar
juice of ½ lemon
2–3 tbsp chopped fresh tarragon

Perfect with light fish and chicken dishes, this can easily be adapted for other seasonal vegetables, such as green beans, leeks and broccoli.

1 Lightly steam or boil the mixed vegetables, starting with the firmer ones like the baby carrots, then adding the sliced courgettes and finally the quickest to cook, the sugar snap peas.
2 Melt a cube of the butter in a small pan. Add the shallots and cook for 3 minutes until softened. Pour in the vinegar and reduce by half. Remove the pan from the heat and carefully whisk in the rest of the butter cubes.
3 Stir in the lemon juice and tarragon. Season with salt and black pepper. Pour over the vegetables.

Cabbage and leeks with mustard seeds

This dish of thinly sliced leeks and cabbage, stir-fried then finished with crème fraîche, is quick and easy to cook... perfect for relaxed entertaining.

Prepare the leeks and cabbage and chill in polythene bags for up to 4 hours.

PREPARATION 10 MINUTES
COOKING 10 MINUTES
SERVES 6

2 tbsp groundnut or sunflower oil
2 tsp black mustard seeds
2 leeks, thinly sliced
600g/1lb 5oz cabbage, finely shredded
3 tbsp crème fraîche

1 Heat the oil in a large frying pan or wok. Tip in the mustard seeds and fry quickly until they sizzle. Add the leeks and stir-fry until the green pieces turn bright green, then add the cabbage and stir-fry for 2–3 minutes, until the cabbage has wilted.
2 Season well with salt and pepper, then splash in 2 tablespoons of water. Cover and cook for a further 2–3 minutes, until the cabbage is tender.
3 Spoon the contents of the pan into a serving dish, pour over the crème fraîche and sprinkle with freshly ground black pepper.

Cauliflower with crispy crumb top

This simple topping of lemon, crumbs and parsley adds a touch of colour and crunch to cauliflower. Serve with any fish, chicken or meat dish; it's also good cold.

Fry the crumbs and parboil the cauliflower a few hours in advance.

PREPARATION 10 MINUTES
COOKING 15 MINUTES
SERVES 6

1 large cauliflower, separated into
  even-sized florets

FOR THE TOPPING
85g/3oz butter
100g/4oz fresh breadcrumbs
1 garlic clove, finely chopped
grated zest of 1 small lemon
2 tbsp chopped fresh parsley

1 Start making the topping: melt 50g/2oz of the butter in a frying pan. When foaming, add the bread-crumbs and fry until crisp and golden, about 5 minutes. Stir in the garlic, then set the pan aside.
2 Steam the cauliflower over a large pan of boiling water for 5 minutes. Heat the rest of the butter in a separate pan, add the cauli-flower and fry until it just starts to brown.
3 Spoon the florets into a hot serving dish. Mix the lemon zest and parsley with the breadcrumbs, season with salt and pepper and sprinkle the mixture over the cauliflower.

Sweet-and-sour onions

Cook the dish the day before. Reheat in a moderate oven for 20–30 minutes.

PREPARATION 20 MINUTES

COOKING 1 HOUR 5 MINUTES

SERVES 6

50g/2oz butter

1 tbsp olive oil

2 tbsp light muscovado sugar

4 tbsp red wine vinegar

900g/2lb baby onions, peeled
  and trimmed

2 bay leaves

4 sprigs of fresh thyme

3 tbsp raisins

3 tbsp pine nuts

These are great with roast lamb or beef. For an even richer caramelized flavour, replace 2 tablespoons of the red wine vinegar with balsamic vinegar. To make peeling onions easier, put the unpeeled onions in a pan of boiling water, simmer for 5 minutes, then drain and cool under running water. The skins should then peel off easily.

1 Melt the butter with the oil in a large ovenproof dish or pan. Add the muscovado sugar and half the vinegar, then tip in the onions (they should be in one layer) and stir to coat them in the hot butter. Scatter over the bay leaves and thyme sprigs. Cook over a medium heat for 20 minutes without stirring.
2 Preheat the oven to 150C/300F/Gas 2. Give the onions a good stir. Add the raisins, pine nuts, the rest of the vinegar and a tablespoon of water; season with salt and pepper. Bake in the oven for 45 minutes until the onions are caramelized. Serve warm.

Sweet potato and celeriac mash

Keep guests guessing about the true identity of this mash. This lovely combination is great with roasts or casseroles as it soaks up sauces beautifully.

Make the mash, put in the dish, cover and chill up to 4 hours in advance. Bake in a moderate oven for 40 minutes.

PREPARATION 10 MINUTES
COOKING 45 MINUTES
SERVES 6

700g/1lb 9oz sweet potatoes (peeled weight)
700g/1lb 9oz celeriac (peeled weight)
142ml/¼ pint carton of single cream
25g/1oz butter
freshly grated nutmeg

1 Preheat the oven to 200C/400F/Gas 6. Cut the vegetables into even-sized chunks and cook in a large pan of boiling salted water for 20–25 minutes until softened. Drain well.

2 Pour the cream into the pan, warm through gently without boiling, then return the potatoes and celeriac to the pan. Turn off the heat and mash the vegetables well. Season generously with salt and pepper.

3 Spoon the mash into a buttered shallow ovenproof dish and form hollows and peaks on the top with the back of a spoon. Dot with butter and grate some nutmeg generously over the top. Bake for 20 minutes from hot or 40 minutes from cold.

VARIATION
For a quick snack, stir in cubes of ham, top with grated cheese and brown it under the grill. Serve with a fresh green salad and sliced tomatoes for a lunchtime snack for 4 people.

THE PERFECT MASH

For 6 people: cut 1.3kg/3lb peeled floury potatoes, such as King Edward, Maris Piper or Cara, into chunks. Cook in boiling salted water until tender right through. Drain well in a colander, then return the potatoes to the pan, cover with a lid and leave to steam and dry off for 5 minutes. Meanwhile, heat 150ml/ $^{1}/_{4}$ pint milk in a small pan with 50g/2oz butter. Mash the potatoes until they are smooth, or put them through a potato ricer, then add the hot milk and butter gradually, mashing all the time. Season well with salt, freshly ground pepper and freshly grated nutmeg.

Golden mash

Cook 900g/2lb floury potatoes and 225g/8oz carrots, peeled and cut into chunks, until tender; drain. Heat 5 tablespoons of milk and a knob of butter until the butter melts; add the potatoes and carrots, and mash well. Stir in a bunch of chopped spring onions; season.

Mix and mash

Spring mint mash: For a light, fresh-tasting mash, omit the butter and milk and add 6 tablespoons of crème fraîche or Greek yoghurt along with 6 tablespoons of finely chopped spring onions and about 4–6 tablespoons of chopped fresh mint.

Garlic or onion mash: Add 3–4 whole, peeled garlic cloves or 1 large onion, chopped, to the boiling potatoes. They will soften and mash in easily for a mild garlic or onion mash. Alternatively, stir-fry finely sliced onion rings and some garlic slivers in olive oil and pile on top of the mash with freshly snipped chives.

Mixed root mash: To about 650g/1lb 7oz peeled potatoes, cut into chunks, add a mixture of carrots and parsnips or sweet potato or swede, all cut into chunks, in any proportion you like, to make the weight up to 1.3kg/3lb. Cook all the vegetables together in the pan, mash well with milk and butter, then add lots of fresh chopped parsley.

Bubble and squeak or green pea mash: Add about 450g /1lb freshly boiled or steamed shredded cabbage to 1kg/ 2lb 4oz of mash, with perhaps a tablespoon of coarsegrain mustard. For a change, add about 450g/1lb frozen peas to 1kg/ 2lb 4oz of boiling potatoes for the last couple of minutes of cooking. Drain and mash them altogether, stirring in some chopped fresh mint.

Blue cheese and bacon mash: Dry-fry or grill 4–6 rashers of streaky bacon (rind removed) until golden and crispy. Chop the bacon and add to the mash along with 3 finely chopped spring onions and 100g/4oz crumbled Stilton or cubes of Dolcelatte cheese. For a vegetarian version, replace the bacon with 50g/2oz toasted walnuts.

Sun-dried tomato, basil and pine nut mash: Instead of adding milk and butter, add 6 tablespoons of extra-virgin olive oil to the mash and stir in 4–6 chopped sun-dried tomatoes. Sprinkle with a generous handful of toasted pine nuts and some freshly torn basil leaves before serving. You could also add a few roasted garlic cloves for an even richer, caramelized flavour.

Tuscan bread and tomatoes

This Italian peasant-style salad, known as Panzanella, relies on the quality of your ingredients – so pick ripe, juicy, tasty tomatoes and use your best extra-virgin olive oil. However, leftover ciabatta is fine for this recipe, as it will crisp up nicely in the oven.

To prepare ahead: dry the bread in the oven and cool.

PREPARATION 15 MINUTES
COOKING 20 MINUTES
SERVES 6 AS A SIDE SALAD

½ ciabatta loaf
900g/2lb ripe tomatoes
1 red onion, thinly sliced
2 garlic cloves, finely chopped
generous bunch of basil leaves

FOR THE DRESSING
6 tbsp extra-virgin olive oil
3 tbsp red wine vinegar

1 Preheat the oven to 180C/350F/Gas 4. Slice the ciabatta fairly thinly, then put the slices on a baking sheet in a single layer. Bake for 10 minutes, then turn the slices over and bake for a further 10 minutes, until the bread is lightly browned and dry. Allow to cool on a wire rack.

2 Cut the tomatoes into small wedges or chop them if they are large. Put them in a large bowl with the onion and garlic. Mix well. Break the bread up into small chunks and add to the bowl. Tear the basil leaves into small pieces and add to the bowl. Mix well.

3 Make the dressing: whisk together the oil, vinegar, salt and pepper. Drizzle the dressing over the salad and mix well. You want the bread to take on the flavours of the basil and oil without getting too soggy, so serve the salad within an hour of making it.

A Chianti Classico makes an elegant partner for this dish. For a more powerful match, choose a red from one of the flying winemakers working in Sicily or Puglia.

COMPOSING SALADS

With a little imagination, virtually any combination goes – hot meat with cool leaves, fusions of cheese, fresh fruit and vegetables, plus any amount of fantastic dressings to give that extra flavour boost. Try adding a few surprise flavours of your own and don't forget to provide plenty of variety of textures. If the salads have a fair share of meat, fish, eggs or cheese in them, they're substantial enough for a main meal.

There are no firm rules about when to serve salads or what to use in them, but the simpler the better. Flavours shouldn't fight each other – try to stick to two or three main ingredients. The most important thing to consider is the quality of your raw ingredients. Always buy the best and freshest you can find and, obviously if the produce is seasonal, it'll be in its prime.

Think ahead

Preparing salad leaves an hour or two before you need them and keeping them in the fridge gives them time to crisp and freshen up. Just wash them, then dry them carefully, in a spinner or by gently patting in tea towels or kitchen paper. Put in plastic containers or plastic bags in the salad drawer of the fridge. Wash fresh herbs and keep them in bags in the fridge. Tear soft-leaved varieties of lettuce or shred the crisper ones with a sharp knife – the leaves are always best bite-sized. Leave dressing salads until the last minute, unless the recipe says otherwise.

Prewashed bagged salads are one of the great innovations of our age. The leaves arrive, in their pillow of air, pristine and bone dry; pricier than dealing with your own, but the results are outstanding.

Essential equipment

You don't really need any special equipment to assemble your salads. However, it is very useful to have a SALAD SPINNER, especially one with a non-slip base that you can spin like a top while the water flies away. If you don't have a spinner, a clean tea towel will soak up the moisture well. For the finest slivers of cucumber, carrot, or whatever vegetable you require, a MANDOLIN is a must. There are wooden or plastic ones, but both are guillotine sharp. The blades can be adjusted to shred or to produce very fine slices through to chunkier ones. Some have a piece of plastic that grips the vegetables, keeping your fingers out of the way. It doesn't take long to learn to use a mandolin – and the results are fast.

A glossary of oils and vinegars

OLIVE OIL – and preferably extra-virgin – is what every salad is crying out for. The best is labelled 'first cold pressing' and is extracted by a natural process and not refined industrially. The greenest is not always the finest – it depends what sort of flavours you want.

Buy small bottles and try them out. As a rule the further north the olives are grown, the lighter the flavour. Italian oils have a light, grassy flavour, balanced by a peppery aftertaste, and Spanish oils are delicate, but with a subtle earthiness. For a more gutsy, pungent oil, pick a Greek one. Just drizzle good olive oil liberally over salads or make a classic vinaigrette. Use a lighter olive oil or mix it with sunflower oil to make mayonnaise.

NUT OILS work well in both simple and complex dressings. They come in small bottles because they have a short shelf-life (and are best used within 3 months of opening). Almond oil has a delicate flavour for light vinaigrettes for fish and vegetable salads. Hazelnut and walnut oils both have rich nutty flavours and both go well with fruity flavoured vinegars or with honey in the dressing, or they are perfect for a dashing drizzle on a green leaf salad if you haven't got time to make a vinaigrette.

SESAME OIL can be cold pressed from fresh seeds, or, more commonly, refined from roasted seeds which gives it a strong taste. It is ideal for Chinese-style salads, but mix it with grapeseed oil for others or it may overpower some ingredients.

GRAPESEED OIL and SUNFLOWER OIL both have a light flavour and can be used when you have chillies and garlic in the salad dressing, or you feel you need to lighten the flavour of stronger oils.

VINEGARS – white and red are essentials for basic salad dressings. They vary in strength and quality, so try a few. Good ones will be labelled with the wine used, and aged in barrels to ensure a rounded flavour. Use white wine vinegar for lighter dressings; red wine vinegar for dressings with mustard, garlic, shallots and nuts. CIDER VINEGAR made from apple juice has a sweet, dominant flavour so use sparingly. Either use a little less or use part cider vinegar and part wine vinegar.

SHERRY VINEGARS have a richer taste, but can really liven up a salad dressing, especially for warm salads. They enjoy being partnered with fruity olive oils and nut oils, the best ones mature in old oak sherry casks for an authentic flavour – check the label on the bottle.

Sweet and richly aromatic, BALSAMIC VINEGAR is made from trebbiano grapes and the best are aged for over 10 years. Since it has become popular, however, the process has been speeded up, which has meant the price has dropped, so we can all enjoy a little splash in salads. Use sparingly, as it is sweet, and omit sugar if there is any in the recipe.

The best RICE VINEGAR comes from Japan and is pale. It works well with all oils to make clean-tasting dressings. You can also find seasoned rice vinegar dressing that can be used directly on salads without adding any oil – if you are cutting down on the fat in your diet. It is also a pleasant mild substitute for wine vinegar.

FLAVOURED VINEGARS, such as raspberry or tarragon in wonderful shaped bottles, have become very popular as gifts. It's easy just to admire them on the shelf, but you'll miss out on a treat if you leave them for too long.

Cos, pea and Parmesan salad

Just a few ingredients, simply served, make this a very chic salad to accompany a grilled fish or meat main course.

To prepare ahead: pod the peas, then blanch. Wash the lettuce, dry and seal in a bag in the fridge.

PREPARATION 10 MINUTES
COOKING 2 MINUTES
SERVES 6 AS A SIDE SALAD

175g/6oz fresh podded peas (450g/1lb pods yield around 175g/6oz peas) or frozen peas
2 medium Cos lettuces
about 25g/1oz fresh Parmesan cheese

FOR THE DRESSING
good handful of fresh mint leaves
1 tbsp golden caster sugar
3 tbsp fresh lemon juice
6 tbsp crème fraîche

1 Bring a pan of water to the boil. Add the peas and cook for 1–2 minutes, depending on their size. Drain and refresh under cold water. Drain again and dry on kitchen paper.

2 Separate the lettuce leaves and keep about 24–36 evenly sized ones whole, then roughly tear up the other leaves.

3 Make the dressing: chop the mint leaves on a board with the sugar. Put the mixture in a bowl and stir in the lemon juice, followed by the crème fraîche.

4 To serve the salad, put 4 to 6 whole lettuce leaves in each individual bowl, then scatter over some torn leaves. Sprinkle with a portion of peas and spoon over some dressing. Finish with shavings of Parmesan, and season with salt and freshly ground black pepper.

Pick a restrained white wine that will not dominate the fresh flavours of this salad. An Italian Pinot Grigio or good-quality Soave make excellent choices.

Pink grapefruit and walnut salad

To prepare ahead: toast the walnuts, segment the grapefruit and wash the rocket leaves.

PREPARATION 15 MINUTES
COOKING 5 MINUTES
SERVES 6 AS A SIDE SALAD

100g/4oz walnut halves, broken
  into smaller pieces
2 pink grapefruit
4 tbsp walnut oil
150g/5oz rocket leaves
150g/5oz feta cheese, crumbled

Delicate and refreshing as a side salad or starter, the tangy flavours of this salad go well with simple main courses of duck, steak, grilled lamb or trout.

1 Preheat the oven to 200C/400F/Gas 6. Tip the walnuts into a baking tray and roast for 5 minutes until the nuts are brown – but watch they don't burn. Put on a plate to cool.
2 Segment the grapefruit: slice off the top and bottom of the fruit and, with a sharp knife, cut off the peel, making sure there is no white pith left. Over a bowl to catch the juices, cut into each segment between the membranes. Halve the fruit segments if they are large.
3 Put the walnut oil into the bowl and stir in the reserved grapefruit juice and fruit segments. Add the rocket leaves, cheese and toasted walnuts and toss gently. Divide between 6 side plates.

This salad demands a full-bodied wine that is not acidic – the grapefruit does that job. So choose a dry sherry, which has the style and character to match the nutty dressing.

VARIATIONS
Instead of the walnuts, use hazelnuts. Instead of grapefruit and walnut oil, use oranges and hazelnut oil. Toss with baby spinach instead of rocket and use a creamy blue cheese instead of the feta.

Warm wild mushroom and duck salad

To prepare ahead: make the dressing up to 2 hours in advance.

PREPARATION 15 MINUTES
COOKING 20 MINUTES
SERVES 6 AS A LIGHT MAIN-COURSE
  SALAD

4 tbsp clear honey
3 duck breasts, each about 175g/6oz
bunch of spring onions
3 tbsp olive oil
2 garlic cloves, finely chopped
650g/1lb 7oz mixed chestnut and wild
  mushrooms, halved
2 bags of lamb's lettuce

FOR THE DRESSING
3 tbsp fresh orange juice
1 tbsp red wine vinegar
5 tbsp olive oil
1 tsp wholegrain mustard
2 tbsp Greek-style yoghurt
1 garlic clove, crushed

Honey-basted duck breasts and wild mushrooms marry so well. This is a very special salad that looks impressive, but is quick and easy to make. Don't soak wild mushrooms in water or they will lose their texture. Instead, use a small brush and damp kitchen paper to wipe them clean.

1 Preheat the grill to high. Brush honey on one side of each duck breast and season. Grill for 10 minutes until caramelized, then repeat on other side. Allow to rest for 5 minutes, then slice each breast into 6 pieces.
2 Slice the spring onions at an angle and chop the green tops.
3 Make the dressing: whisk all the ingredients together, adding the spring onion greens.
4 Heat a large frying pan, add the oil and garlic and fry for 1 minute. Add the mushrooms and stir-fry for 5 minutes. Bubble off any excess liquid. Remove from the heat and add the spring onions. Season.
5 Divide the lettuce between 6 plates. Top each with mushrooms and 3 duck slices. Drizzle with dressing.

An ideal match for this special dish is an elegant German Riesling. Choose the best quality you can afford from the Nahe or Rheingau wine regions.

Potato and pastrami salad

This is a versatile salad for parties and picnics, easily made in large quantities. It can be served as a main meal, or omit the pastrami and serve as a side salad. In season (May to July), beetroot can be eaten raw, but later it can get woody, so it must be cooked. You can buy it ready-cooked in vacuum packs (avoid those bottled in vinegar).

Make the salad the day before, cover and chill. Grate the beetroot 2 hours ahead, cover and chill.

PREPARATION 15 MINUTES
COOKING 15 MINUTES
SERVES 6 AS A MAIN-COURSE SALAD

900g/2lb small new potatoes or salad potatoes, scrubbed and sliced
1 can of anchovy fillets, drained, rinsed and roughly chopped
2 tbsp capers, roughly chopped
1–2 tbsp horseradish sauce
4 large fresh dill sprigs
24 thin pastrami slices
1 raw or cooked beetroot (about 100g/4oz), peeled

FOR THE DRESSING
2 tbsp white wine vinegar
6 tbsp olive oil

1 Cook the potatoes in boiling salted water for 12–15 minutes until tender. Drain well. Put half of them in a bowl and mash roughly.

2 Make the dressing by whisking the vinegar and oil together. Add half to the mashed potato along with the anchovies, capers and horseradish sauce; season.

3 Add the potato slices and the leaves from 2 dill sprigs. Mix carefully so as not to break up the potatoes.

4 Arrange the pastrami on each plate. Serve with the potato salad. Grate the beetroot into a bowl, add a spoonful of the remaining dressing and stir to coat. Spoon on top of the potato salad. Drizzle over the remaining dressing and sprinkle with the rest of the dill.

A light-bodied red works well with the lively flavours of this salad. Go French and pick a Cabernet Franc-based red from the Loire, or for a more fruity style, a Cru Beaujolais.

Desserts

The pudding is now making a comeback –
but with a serious touch of luxury. It can be
embellished with all manner of extras – a
splash of alcohol, extra cream or exotic fruits
and spices or a good-quality dark chocolate.
However, desserts needn't be elaborate creations.
For a last-minute supper with friends, a few
choice fresh seasonal fruits and a bowl of softly
whipped cream, or an interesting cheese platter,
would be perfect. Try serving a creamy dip
alongside fruit, such as cream whipped with
lime or a liqueur and a little sugar to sweeten,
or a smooth chocolate sauce.

Whisky bread and butter pudding

To prepare ahead: arrange the buttered bread in the dish. Make and chill the custard, and weigh out the fruit and nuts, up to 4 hours ahead.

PREPARATION 10 MINUTES
COOKING 1 HOUR
SERVES 6

50g/2oz butter
1 small French stick, cut into 12 slices
4 tbsp whisky
150g/5oz seedless raisins
100g/4oz pecan halves
5 eggs
100g/4oz light muscovado sugar
1 litre/1³/₄ pints full-fat milk
284ml/¹/₂ pint carton of whipping cream
2 tsp vanilla extract
¹/₂ tsp ground cinnamon
¹/₄ tsp freshly grated nutmeg

Our creamy, boozy version of this perennially popular pudding is really special.

A bain-marie is a water bath used to control the heat when cooking certain foods that are sensitive to direct heat, such as egg custards; it helps prevent them curdling or going grainy. Put the dish (or moulds) in a roasting tin and pour in enough warm water to come about two-thirds up the sides. The water should never get hotter than a gentle simmer, so the custard will set but still be creamy.

1 Preheat the oven to 180C/350F/Gas 4. Butter a 33 x 23cm/13 x 9in ovenproof dish (6cm/2¹/₂in deep). Butter each bread slice on one side. Arrange, butter-side up, in the dish. Drizzle over the whisky.
2 Scatter over the raisins and pecan halves. Beat the eggs in a bowl, then mix in the sugar. Stir in the milk, cream and vanilla. Pour the mixture over the bread and sprinkle with the spices.
3 Stand the dish in a bain-marie and bake for 50–60 minutes, until just set, golden and crisp.

Plum and banana crumbles

To prepare ahead: cook the crumble mixture the night before. Cool, then keep in a sealed plastic bag. Once the crumbles are assembled, return them to the oven for 10 minutes.

PREPARATION 20 MINUTES
COOKING 30 MINUTES
SERVES 6

2 bananas, thickly sliced
1 tbsp lemon juice
700g/1lb 9oz ripe plums, stoned and quartered
4 cardamom pods
50g/2oz golden caster sugar
pouring cream or custard, to serve

FOR THE CRUMBLE TOPPING
85g/3oz butter
100g/4oz plain flour
50g/2oz golden caster sugar
50g/2oz hazelnuts, roughly chopped

Cardamom adds a delicate scent to these delightful individual crumbles.

1 Preheat the oven to 180C/350F/Gas 4. Toss the banana in the lemon juice, then gently mix with the plums. Slit open the cardamom pods and remove the seeds. Crush the seeds using a pestle and mortar. Stir into the plums and bananas with the sugar.
2 Divide the mixture between six 225ml/8fl oz ovenproof dishes. Put on a baking sheet and bake for 30 minutes until the fruit is tender.
3 Meanwhile, make the topping: rub the butter into the flour until it resembles crumbs. Stir in the sugar and nuts and tip on to a baking sheet in an even layer. Cook for 20–25 minutes until golden.
4 Break up the crumble mixture a little and spoon some over the fruit in each dish. Serve at once with pouring cream or custard.

VARIATIONS
Seasonal fruits add a special touch. Gooseberries, blackberries or greengages (August/early September), or damsons (September) would work particularly well.

THE PERFECT CUSTARD

Traditional egg custard is a delicious and versatile sauce. Cold, it forms the basis of many desserts, like ice-cream. Warm, it's the perfect accompaniment to any hot pudding.

Vanilla custard
Preparation 5 minutes
Cooking 10 minutes
Serves 6

1 vanilla pod
300ml/½ pint full-fat milk
4 egg yolks
25g/1oz golden caster sugar

1 Split the vanilla pod lengthwise and scrape the seeds into a pan, then add the pod. Pour in the milk and bring to the boil slowly, pressing the pod and seeds with a wooden spoon

to release as much flavour as possible, then simmer very gently for about 5 minutes.
2 In a bowl, whisk the egg yolks and sugar until thick and pale. Strain the hot milk through a fine sieve into a jug, then pour into the egg mixture in a steady stream, whisking all the time so the yolks don't scramble.
3 Pour back into the pan and cook over a low heat, stirring constantly, for about 2–3 minutes until smooth and thick enough to coat the back of a spoon (don't let it boil).
4 Serve warm, or allow to cool and chill if serving cold. Cover the top closely with plastic film to prevent a skin forming.

Variations

Leave out the vanilla pod and add any of the following:

Chocolate – Add 25g/1oz grated dark chocolate to the simmering milk and whisk well until smooth.
Lemon or orange – Use a vegetable peeler to cut 6 large strips of peel (avoiding the white pith) from a lemon or orange. Add to the milk in the pan and heat slowly to release the flavour. Pour the milk through a fine sieve into the egg mixture. You could also add a dash of Grand Marnier to the cooled custard, if you like.
Cardamom – Split 3 large cardamom pods, discard the husks and lightly crush the seeds. Add to the milk for a lovely scented flavour. Serve with poached fruits.
Ginger – Add 1 finely chopped piece of stem ginger to the cooked custard. This is delicious with apple pie or any dried fruit pudding.

Baked Alaska

In summer, use whatever fruits are in season and a liqueur to match –
for example, cherries and kirsch; at other times, use a pack of mixed
frozen berries.

To prepare ahead: macerate the fruit
overnight.

PREPARATION 20 MINUTES, PLUS
  CHILLING AND MACERATING
COOKING 5 MINUTES
SERVES 8

500g/1lb 2 oz bag of frozen summer
  fruits, defrosted and drained
4 tbsp crème de cassis
300g/10oz Madeira cake
two 500ml/18 fl oz tubs of Pecan Toffee
  Crunch ice-cream, or similar flavour,
  softened in the fridge for 20 minutes
whites of 4 large eggs
225g/8oz golden caster sugar

1 Put the summer fruits in a bowl and stir in the cassis. Cover and
leave to macerate for at least 2 hours, or preferably overnight.
2 Cut the cake in half widthwise, then cut each half lengthwise into 3
slices. Lay the cake slices on a flat ovenproof dish or plate to form one
large rectangle. Spoon the fruit and juices into the centre of each slice.
Carefully take the ice-cream out of the tubs, trying to keep whole, and sit
each tubful on top of the fruit sponge base. Press the two ice-creams
together into a rectangular shape, leaving a 2.5cm/1in border of sponge.
Level the top, then return to the freezer for about 20 minutes until the
ice-cream is firm again. Preheat the oven to 230C/450F/Gas 8.
3 In a large grease-free bowl, whisk the egg whites to soft peaks.
Whisk in the sugar, a couple of tablespoons at a time, until the
mixture is stiff and glossy.
4 Spoon this meringue over the ice-cream and sponge as quickly as
possible, enclosing it completely; swirl into peaks. Bake for about 5
minutes until the meringue starts to brown. Serve immediately.

Cointreau crêpes

To prepare ahead: fill and fold the pancakes, make the sauce, and segment and chill the oranges earlier in the day.

PREPARATION 10 MINUTES
COOKING 25 MINUTES
SERVES 6

85g/3oz unsalted butter, softened
3 tbsp Cointreau
12 home-made or ready-made
   pancakes
whipped cream, to serve

FOR THE SAUCE
grated zest and juice of 2 oranges
grated zest of 1 lemon
85g/3oz golden caster sugar
2 tbsp brandy or rum
3 oranges, segmented

This is based on the classic crêpes suzette, normally cooked at the last minute. Spreading them with flavoured butter means baking them is much easier.

1 Preheat the oven to 190C/375F/Gas 5. In a bowl, mix together the butter and Cointreau and spread a little over each pancake. Fold the pancakes into quarters and arrange them in a shallow ovenproof dish.
2 Make the sauce: in a large bowl, mix together the orange zest and juice, lemon zest, caster sugar and brandy or rum.
3 Pour the sauce over the pancakes, cover the dish with foil and cook the pancakes in the oven for 20 minutes. Add the orange segments, cover again and return to the oven for 5 minutes more.
4 Serve the crêpes with whipped cream.

Coconut soufflé with spiced pineapple

This soufflé has a really tropical flavour. Sweetened, tenderized, shredded coconut is available in most supermarkets and is ideal for this dish.

1 Well ahead, make the spiced pineapple: gently heat the sugar with 85ml/3fl oz water, stirring until dissolved. Add the lemon zest and cinnamon, and simmer for 2 minutes. Stir in the lemon juice and leave to cool. Pour over the pineapple in a shallow non-metallic dish, cover and leave for 4–6 hours.

2 Preheat the oven to 200C/400F/Gas 6. Butter a 15 x 9cm/6 x 3½in soufflé dish and sprinkle in a little sugar to coat.

3 Mix the milk and coconut cream. Melt the butter in a pan and stir in the flour. Cook for 1–2 minutes, stirring. Remove from the heat and gradually stir in the milk. Bring to the boil, stirring, then simmer for 1 minute. Stir in the sugar, lime zest and shredded coconut. Let cool slightly, then mix in the egg yolks.

4 Whisk the egg whites until stiff. Fold a tablespoonful into the coconut mixture to lighten. Fold in the rest and spoon the mixture into the dish.

5 Bake for 30–35 minutes until risen and golden. Sprinkle with lime zest, if you like, and serve with the pineapple in its syrup.

To prepare ahead: macerate the pineapple slices the night before. No more than 2 hours ahead, make the soufflé mixture up to the end of step 4, cover with plastic film and chill.

PREPARATION 15 MINUTES, PLUS 4–6
   HOURS' MACERATING
COOKING 20–25 MINUTES
SERVES 6

50g/2oz butter, plus extra
85g/3oz golden caster sugar,
   plus extra
100ml/3½fl oz milk
200ml/7 fl oz carton of coconut cream
50g/2oz flour
grated zest of 1 lime, plus more for
   decoration (optional)
50g/2oz shredded coconut
4 eggs, separated

FOR THE SPICED PINEAPPLE
85g/3oz caster sugar
pared zest and juice of 1 lemon
1 cinnamon stick
1 small sweet (golden) pineapple,
   peeled and cut into 6 wedges

Baked nectarines and cherries

To prepare ahead: flavour the mascarpone and stone the cherries the day before. Scrape the seeds from the vanilla pod and mix with the orange juice.

PREPARATION 15 MINUTES
COOKING 25–30 MINUTES
SERVES 4–6

4–6 nectarines or peaches, halved
  and stoned
225g/8oz cherries, stoned
85g/3oz unrefined demerara sugar
1 vanilla pod
juice of 2 large oranges

FOR THE BRANDIED MASCARPONE
250g/9oz tub of mascarpone
25g/1oz icing sugar
2 tbsp brandy

Baked fruits are a simple but delicious summer dessert and the brandied mascarpone makes a luxurious accompaniment. Serve as part of an Italian meal.

1 Preheat the oven to 200C/400F/ Gas 6. Arrange the nectarines or peaches, cut-side up, in a shallow ovenproof dish and scatter the cherries around them and in the hollows. Sprinkle with the sugar. Split the vanilla pod almost in half lengthwise and scrape out the seeds. Mix the vanilla seeds with the orange juice and pour over the fruit. Bake for 25–30 minutes until the fruit is tender.

2 Meanwhile, make the brandied mascarpone: put the mascarpone in a small bowl and beat until smooth. Stir in the icing sugar and brandy.

3 When the fruits are cooked, divide them between 4 or 6 serving bowls and serve with a spoonful of the brandied mascarpone.

Bake the tart the day before, cool, wrap in plastic film and keep at room temperature; or make a month in advance, wrap in plastic film, seal, label and freeze. Thaw at room temperature overnight.

PREPARATION 20 MINUTES, PLUS
  CHILLING
COOKING 50 MINUTES
SERVES 8

FOR THE PASTRY
175g/6oz plain flour
100g/4oz butter, cut into cubes
50g/2oz caster sugar
1 egg yolk
5 tbsp apricot jam, for the glaze

FOR THE FILLING
200g/7oz ready-to-eat, pitted prunes
5 tbsp brandy or Armagnac
175g/6oz marzipan
50g/2oz caster sugar
85g/3oz butter
25g/1oz plain flour
2 eggs

Prune and marzipan tart

Rich and stylish, our version of this classic French tart uses ready-made marzipan. Use Agen prunes if you can find them. From the Bordeaux region of France, these are considered to be the finest dessert prunes. Hence they are fairly expensive and can only be found in larger supermarkets and delicatessens. The dried ready-to-eat prunes from California are good too. Also go for good-quality marzipan – white is invariably better than golden.

1 Preheat oven to 200C/400F/Gas 6. Put the flour and butter in a food processor and mix into crumbs. Add the sugar and mix briefly. Add the egg yolk, 1–2 tablespoons of cold water and pulse or mix briefly to form a firm dough. Wrap in plastic film and chill for 30 minutes.
2 Make the filling: soak the prunes in 2 tablespoons of the brandy while the pastry is resting. Chop the marzipan into small pieces and put in the food processor with the sugar and butter. Work until soft, then add the flour and eggs.
3 Roll out the pastry to line a 23–24cm/9–9½in flan tin. Trim the edges and bake blind for 10 minutes. Remove the paper and beans and bake for 5 minutes more. Remove from oven and allow to cool slightly. Reduce the oven setting to 180C/350F/Gas 4.
4 Spread 2 tablespoons of the jam over the pastry. Spread the marzipan cream over the top (pic. 1). Arrange the prunes and liquid evenly over the filling (pic. 2). Bake for 30–35 minutes until risen and golden. Allow to cool in the tin, then transfer to a large serving plate.
5 Heat the remaining jam and brandy together, stirring, until syrupy. Brush over the tart and serve warm or cold.

Goats' cheese, pear and blackberry tart

Soft goats' cheese has a mild, but subtly piquant, flavour. A slice of
this tart combines cheese and fruit with the dessert course.

To prepare ahead: take the pastry out
of the freezer the night before to thaw.

PREPARATION 15 MINUTES
COOKING 25–30 MINUTES
SERVES 6

375g/13oz sheet of ready-rolled puff
  pastry, defrosted if frozen
85g/3oz soft goats' cheese or curd
  cheese
3 ripe pears, quartered, cored and
  each sliced into 3
1 tbsp lemon juice
175g/6oz blackberries
25g/1oz golden caster sugar
2 tbsp clear honey

1 Preheat the oven to 200C/400F/Gas 6. Open out the pastry sheet
and lay it on a large baking sheet. Trim the pastry edges with a sharp
knife so the sheet measures just over 33 x 20cm/13 x 8in. Lightly
score a border all round the edge with the back of a knife, taking care
not to cut right through (this creates an attractive puffed-up border
all the way round which keeps all the fruity juices contained).
2 Spread the goats' cheese over the pastry inside the border. Toss
the pear slices in the lemon juice and scatter them over the goats'
cheese, then top with the blackberries and sprinkle over the sugar.
3 Bake for 25–30 minutes, until the pastry is golden and cooked
through. Drizzle with honey just before serving, cut into 6 pieces.

Sticky date pudding with caramel sauce

PREPARATION 15 MINUTES
COOKING 2 HOURS
SERVES 8

100g/4oz softened butter, plus more
  for the pudding basin and paper
175g/6oz dates
100g/4oz light muscovado sugar
2 eggs, lightly beaten
$\frac{1}{2}$ tsp vanilla extract
175g/6oz self-raising flour,
  plus 1 rounded tbsp
4 tbsp milk

FOR THE SAUCE
150g/5oz light muscovado sugar
142ml/$\frac{1}{4}$ pint carton of double cream
100g/4oz butter
$\frac{1}{2}$ tsp vanilla extract

1 Butter a 1.4 litre/$2\frac{1}{2}$ pint pudding basin. Halve, stone and chop the dates.
2 In a bowl, beat together the butter and sugar until light and fluffy. Beat in the eggs, a little at a time. Add the vanilla, then fold in the flour and milk to give a soft, dropping consistency. Stir in the chopped dates.
3 Spoon the mixture into the pudding basin and smooth the top. Cover with a piece of buttered greaseproof paper, then foil, folding a 2.5cm/1in pleat in each to allow the pudding to rise and sealing well. Steam for 2 hours, checking that the water is constantly boiling and topping up with more boiling water every half hour if necessary, until risen and firm.
4 Make the sauce: put all the ingredients in a small pan and bring to the boil, stirring. Simmer for 5 minutes until thickened.
5 Serve the pudding with the sauce.

Lemon and apple bavarois

Make the day before; chill. Make the crisps up to 2 days ahead; store airtight.

PREPARATION 30 MINUTES, PLUS
  OVERNIGHT CHILLING
COOKING 1½ HOURS
SERVES 6

11g sachet of powdered gelatine
450g/1lb Bramley apples, peeled,
  cored and chopped
2–3 tbsp caster sugar
2 lemons
400ml/14fl oz carton of ready-made
  custard
142ml/¼ pint carton of double cream
whites of 2 eggs, at room temperature

FOR THE APPLE CRISPS
200g/7oz golden granulated sugar
1 lemon
2 Granny Smiths, whole

1 The day before: measure 3 tablespoons of cold water into a bowl, sprinkle in the gelatine and leave to soak. Put the chopped apples and 2 tablespoons of sugar in a pan with the juice of one of the lemons. Cover and cook for 5 minutes, stirring a few times, until softened. Sieve to make a purée. Taste for sweetness and add a little more sugar if necessary, then allow to cool.

2 Put the gelatine bowl in a small pan with a little water and heat gently until dissolved. Spoon the custard into a large bowl and stir in the gelatine. Mix in the apple purée and grated zest of both lemons. Whip the cream and fold it in.

3 Whisk the egg whites to soft peaks and fold them in. Pour into a 1 litre/1¾ pint basin or mould, cover with film and chill overnight.

4 Make the crisps: preheat the oven to 110C/230F/Gas ¼. Put the sugar in a pan with 400ml/14fl oz water, the grated zest of the lemon and a squeeze of its juice. Heat gently, stirring, until the sugar dissolves. Bring to the boil slowly, then boil rapidly for 5 minutes. Remove from the heat.

5 Thinly slice the apples and add to the syrup for 2 minutes. Remove with a draining spoon and lay on baking sheets. Bake for 1½ hours, then leave to cool on a wire rack.

6 Spoon the bavarois into bowls or tumblers and decorate with the apple crisps.

Melting chocolate puddings

Inspired by Jean-Christophe Novelli's recipe, these rich puddings make
a glorious surprise finale – the centre oozes a rich chocolate sauce as
your spoon goes in. If your oven is on the hot side, check the puddings
after 10 minutes – if they rise too much and crack, they won't ooze as
much sauce.

1 Preheat the oven to 180C/350F/Gas 4. Butter six 175ml/6fl oz dariole
moulds and sit them on a baking sheet.
2 Put the butter and chocolate in a heatproof bowl and set over a pan
of simmering water (or melt in the microwave on High for 3 minutes).
Stir occasionally until melted, then set aside.
3 Using an electric hand whisk, whisk together the eggs, extra yolks
and sugar for about 3 minutes until pale. With the hand blender set to
medium, whisk in the melted chocolate. Gently fold in the flour, then
divide between the moulds.
4 Bake for 10–12 minutes until risen but still flat on top and not
quite firm. Loosen the edges with a round-bladed knife and turn out
immediately. Serve with ice-cream or cream.

To prepare ahead: make the mixture
the day before and spoon into the
moulds. Cover with plastic film and
chill. If left in the fridge for 1 day, then
cook for 15 minutes. The uncooked
puddings can be frozen in their
moulds. To serve, cook from frozen
for about 25 minutes.

PREPARATION 20 MINUTES
COOKING 12–15 MINUTES
SERVES 6

150g/5oz unsalted butter, plus a
    little more for greasing
150g/5oz good-quality plain
    chocolate, roughly chopped
3 eggs, plus extra 3 yolks
85g/3oz golden caster sugar
25g/1oz plain flour, plus 1 rounded
    tbsp
vanilla ice-cream or cream, to serve

Christmas chocolate roulade

The ultimate Swiss roll – with a rich mousse-like texture, indulgent cream filling and special festive decoration. At other times of the year, use small bay leaves instead of holly.

To get ahead, make earlier in the day, chill and fill. Chill until about 30 minutes before serving.

PREPARATION 20 MINUTES, PLUS
  COOLING
COOKING 20 MINUTES
SERVES 8

175g/6oz plain chocolate
5 eggs, separated
175g/6oz caster sugar
284ml/½ pint carton of double cream
2 tbsp Irish cream liqueur
icing sugar, for dusting
chocolate-coated holly leaves or other
  suitable chocolate decorations

1 Preheat the oven to 180C/350F/ Gas 4. Line a 33 x 23cm/13 x 9in Swiss roll tin with non-stick parchment. Melt the plain chocolate in a bowl set over a pan of hot water or in the microwave on High for about 2½ minutes.

2 Put the egg yolks and sugar in a bowl over a pan of simmering water and whisk with an electric hand whisk until the mixture leaves a trail when the blades are lifted, about 5 minutes. Whisk in the melted chocolate.

3 In a large bowl, whisk the egg whites to stiff peaks. Whisk a large spoonful into the chocolate mixture, then fold in the rest.

4 Pour the mixture into the tin and shake gently to spread the mixture into the corners. Bake for 20 minutes until firm. Remove from the oven and leave to cool in the tin, covered loosely with greaseproof paper or foil, for about 3 hours.

5 Whip the cream until it just holds its shape, then stir in the liqueur. Put a large sheet of greaseproof paper on the work surface, turn out the roulade and remove the backing paper. With a short side towards you, mark an indent across the top 2.5cm/1in in. Spread with the cream, then, using the clean greaseproof paper, roll up the roulade.

6 Dust with icing sugar and decorate with chocolate-coated holly leaves.

Mango and coconut terrine

A fruity sorbet with creamy coconut ice-cream, all in one slice. Served with a fresh lime and strawberry sauce, it looks very impressive. The ice-creams need overnight freezing, so start preparation the day before.

The terrine can be made and frozen up to a month in advance. Transfer to the fridge 30 minutes before slicing. Make the sauce up to 2 hours in advance.

PREPARATION 30 MINUTES, PLUS
  OVERNIGHT CHILLING AND FREEZING
COOKING 15 MINUTES
SERVES 8–10

FOR THE MANGO ICE
2 ripe mangoes
50g/2oz caster sugar
3–4 tbsp lime juice

FOR THE COCONUT ICE-CREAM
400ml/14fl oz can of coconut milk
2 large egg yolks
50g/2oz caster sugar
1 tsp cornflour
142ml/¼ pint carton of double cream

FOR THE LIME AND STRAWBERRY SAUCE
100g/4oz unrefined caster sugar
grated zest of 1 lime, plus the juice from 2
200g /7oz strawberries, hulled and sliced

1 Make the mango ice: peel the mangoes and roughly chop the flesh (pic. 1); you need about 550–600g/1lb 3oz–1lb 5oz. Put in a pan with the sugar and 3 tablespoons of water. Simmer for 5-10 minutes. Remove from the heat and blend to a purée in a food processor. Add lime juice to taste. Pour into a plastic container and allow to cool.

2 Make the coconut ice-cream: heat the coconut milk gently in a pan. Beat the yolks and sugar until creamy, then beat in the cornflour. Pour on the hot milk; return to the pan and stir over a medium heat until it is thick enough to coat the back of a spoon (pic. 2). Pour into a bowl, cover with plastic film, allow to cool and then chill.

3 Whip the cream and then fold into the cooled custard. Pour into a plastic container, cover and freeze alongside the mango ice. Leave both for 4 hours until half frozen.

4 Line a 900g/2lb loaf tin with freezer film. Whip the mango ice until smooth and spoon into the tin. Whip the coconut ice to smooth and spread over the top (pic. 3). Cover with freezer film and freeze overnight.

5 Make the sauce: heat the sugar, lime juice and 125ml/4fl oz water in a small pan until the sugar dissolves. Bring to the boil and boil rapidly for 5 minutes until reduced. Remove from heat. Let cool for 5 minutes, then add the lime zest and strawberries. Leave to cool.

6 Transfer the terrine to the fridge about 30 minutes before serving. Turn out on to a plate, slice and serve with the sauce.

Panna cotta with Cointreau sauce

Make the puddings and the sauce the day before and keep chilled.

PREPARATION 20 MINUTES, PLUS
  OVERNIGHT CHILLING
COOKING 10 MINUTES
SERVES 6

2¼ sheets of leaf gelatine
4 tbsp milk
700ml/1¼ pints single cream
1 vanilla pod
50g/2oz caster sugar
150g/5oz raspberries, to serve

FOR THE SAUCE
3 oranges
100g/4oz caster sugar
1 tbsp Cointreau

These softly set puddings are so silky smooth they slip down beautifully at the end of a meal. The fruits can be varied according to the season. As panna cotta requires overnight chilling, you have to start preparation the day before.

1 Break the gelatine into a wide shallow bowl. Pour over the milk and leave to stand for 5 minutes.
2 Pour the cream into a small pan. Split the vanilla pod and scrape the seeds into the cream. Chop the pod and drop into the cream. Stir in the sugar. Heat over a low heat, stirring to dissolve the sugar, until almost boiling. Remove and discard the pieces of vanilla pod.
3 The gelatine will look wrinkled and will have soaked up most of the milk. Stir this into the cream until fully dissolved. Allow to cool slightly, about 10 minutes, then pour the mixture into six 125ml/4fl oz moulds or ramekins (9cm/3½in across). Allow to cool and then chill overnight.
4 Make the sauce: segment 2 of the oranges, saving the juice. Set the segments aside. Squeeze the juice from the third orange, then strain all the juice into a small pan. Add the sugar and heat gently, stirring until dissolved. Bring to the boil then boil until reduced to a syrup, about 2 minutes. Stir in the Cointreau and orange segments. Leave to cool.
5 Loosen the panna cottas from the edge of the dishes with the tip of a knife. Dip the bases very briefly in hot water, then invert on to serving plates. Spoon around the orange segments and sauce, and scatter over some raspberries.

Summer fruits jelly

Using frozen fruits – whether bought or home frozen – means this jelly
is simple to make and quick to set, and makes a fast refreshing treat
at any time of year.

Make and chill up to 4 hours in
advance. As this dessert is made with
frozen fruit it should be eaten on the
same day, as the gradual thawing of
the frozen fruit softens the jelly. To
make a day ahead, first thaw the fruit,
drain off the juices, then make them up
to 600ml/1 pint with the cranberry and
raspberry juice. Alternatively, use fresh
fruits in season.

PREPARATION 5 MINUTES, PLUS
  SETTING
COOKING 5 MINUTES
MAKES 6

600ml/1 pint cranberry and raspberry
  juice (from a carton)
1 tbsp powdered gelatine or 3 gelatine
  leaves
250g/9oz frozen mixed summer fruits
142ml/¼ pint carton of double cream,
  lightly whipped, to serve
biscuits, such as sablés or amaretti,
  to serve

1 Pour the fruit juice into a pan and heat until almost boiling. Take
off the heat.
2 If using powdered gelatine, sprinkle the gelatine over the juice and
whisk well until it dissolves, then leave to cool to room temperature.
If using gelatine leaves, break into a wide shallow bowl, pour over 4
tablespoons of the juice and let stand for 5 minutes. Pour the remaining
juice into a pan and heat. Stir in the gelatine and leave to cool as above.
3 Divide the fruits between 6 glass tumblers and pour the cooled
cranberry liquid over to cover the fruit. Chill until firm.
4 To serve, top each glass with a spoonful of whipped double cream,
and accompany with a few dessert biscuits.

Tiramisu gâteau

This creative variation on the popular Italian trifle makes a very impressive dessert. It is great for entertaining as it can be made the day before, and it also slices very easily to serve a large gathering.

To prepare ahead: make the whole gâteau and chill overnight, or make a month in advance and freeze it in the tin, overwrapped in plastic film. Thaw overnight in the fridge.

PREPARATION 20 MINUTES, PLUS
   OVERNIGHT CHILLING
SERVES 10

175g/6oz good-quality dark chocolate
about 300g/10oz Madeira cake
150ml/¼ pint strong black coffee
5 tbsp Tia Maria, dark rum or brandy
3 x 250g/9oz tubs mascarpone cheese
85g/3oz caster sugar
425ml/¾ pint double cream
85g/3oz amaretti biscuits
icing sugar, for dusting

1 Using a swivel potato peeler, make chocolate curls from about one-third of the chocolate. Coarsely grate the rest.
2 Line the base and sides of a 20cm/8in round, loose-based cake tin with plastic film. Cut the cake into 20 thin slices and use half to line the bottom of the tin, cutting the cake to fit neatly so there are no gaps.
3 Mix the coffee with the Tia Maria, rum or brandy and sprinkle about one-third of the liquid evenly over the cake. Beat together two of the tubs of mascarpone with 50g/2oz of the sugar. Whip 300ml/½ pint of the cream and fold into the cheese. Spoon half this mixture over the cake base, spreading it evenly with the back of a metal spoon. Sprinkle with half the grated chocolate. Crumble the amaretti biscuits into small pieces and scatter evenly over the chocolate. Sprinkle over another third of the coffee liqueur, then the remaining mascarpone mixture and the rest of the grated chocolate.
4 Cover with the last pieces of Madeira cake, again cutting to fit. Sprinkle with the rest of the coffee. Cover the top with plastic film and chill overnight. Chill the chocolate curls on a separate plate, covered loosely with plastic film.
5 Up to 2 hours before serving, uncover the cake and invert it on to a flat serving plate. Carefully remove the tin and peel off the plastic film.
6 Soften the remaining mascarpone, with the remaining sugar. Whip the rest of the cream and fold into the cheese. Spread this mixture over the top and sides of the cake, then sprinkle the top with the chocolate curls. Dust lightly with icing sugar and cut into slices to serve.

Unless you are a confident, gregarious chef who likes to gather their guests around them as they cook, the first thing to ensure in your plan is that not too many dishes need more than the briefest of last-minute attention. Remember that people come to enjoy your company as much as your food. It's no fun for them if they stand around making uncomfortable conversation while you disappear for hours in the kitchen.

Make yourself a countdown – then you will know exactly when you will have to do things. In this way, there will be no danger of being absorbed in pre-dinner-drink chat when you should be putting your main course into the oven and, in fact, you can plan ahead to have plenty of time with your guests before you eat. Writing a countdown in advance will also alert to you to other potential problems, such as too many things having to go in the oven at the same time or needing to be cooked at different temperatures, or of having too many pans on the go at the same time.

Also on the advanced planning front, don't be shy about finding out your guests' likes and dislikes, allergies, vegetarianism, etc. ahead of time. In this way, you can not only avoid potential embarrassment at the table but you can actually build your menu around them rather than, say, having to cook them separate dishes at the last minute. Also, being armed with such knowledge allows you to get beyond the usual entertaining pitfall of playing safe and you will be free to explore more exciting areas such as exotic and spicy food.

A good meal should be a balance of food groups to make it appetizing – and digestible. Try not to repeat ingredients or textures in different courses. Instead, aim to ensure that the meal has a variety of ingredients, colours and textures throughout each course. If the starter is a pastry tartlet, don't follow it with a pie; if soufflés begin the meal, avoid frothy desserts such as egg-based sauces, zabagliones or syllabubs; and if your first course is creamy choose a main course that isn't. Your shopping list will provide good early-warning signals – if you seem to need a lot of eggs, cream or whatever, your menu is probably unbalanced.

The starter should offset the main course, and provide your menu with variety and contrast – serve a fish starter when the main course is meat or poultry, a light one when the main course is weighty, a hot dish before a cold main course or buffet, or something vivid in colour to precede a darkly rich and meaty stew. After a substantial starter, such as the Pork and duck rillettes (page 35) or the Stilton pâté with celery and walnut salad (page 29), go for a lighter main course, such as fish with a light sauce.

To add variety to a meal, avoid serving any vegetables used in the starter as an accompaniment to a main course. It also pays to be flexible when choosing fresh vegetables for accompaniments. First,

take into account what's in season, then more importantly choose what looks in peak condition in your local supermarket or greengrocer's. If you find some really stunning produce, such as new season asparagus, you may want to adjust your first main course to accommodate it.

French restaurants often serve a small, light leafy salad before the starter to your meal because its freshness gets the appetite in gear, and it means serving fewer, if any, vegetables with the main course. You could easily try this out yourself with the suggestions we have for side salads, or some of the cold starters. You can choose to serve a side salad instead of hot vegetables, as long as it enhances the dish and complements the flavours without being too overpowering. If you're serving a salad for a main course, you could keep the whole meal light and summery with a cold starter or, on a chilly day, serve a hot soup like Roasted red pepper soup or Cream of pumpkin soup (pages 13 and 14).

While a cheese course is perfect for certain occasions, remember it will be less appetizing if the meal starts with the Stilton pâté or if you decide to serve the Caesar salad in a Parmesan crust (page 41), but, as long as the meal is not following a strict Oriental theme, it would provide a great contrast after the Thai prawn salad (page 31).

The last course can be as simple or as complex as the rest of the meal allows. After a hefty main course, delicate puddings, such as sorbets, fruit-filled meringues, soufflés or mousses, make a welcome finish. Alternatively, try a fresh fruit salad or a baked fruit pudding. In general, it is usually best to avoid heavy or rich puddings. For a last-minute informal supper, fresh seasonal fruits served with a bowl of softly whipped cream would be the perfect choice. The choice of fruit for a fresh fruit platter should reflect the season. Try serving a creamy dip to accompany it, such as mascarpone or cream whipped with lime juice or a liqueur and a little sugar to sweeten it, or perhaps a smooth chocolate sauce.

The beauty of having a cold dessert waiting in the fridge is that you can relax while your guests are enjoying the main course, happy in the knowledge that pudding is taken care of. Hot puddings, especially home-made ones, are a real treat for entertaining. Just have all the ingredients weighed and as much preparation as possible done ahead of time and you won't have to disappear into the kitchen for too long on the night. There's no need to hurry, however; it's a good idea to give your guests a bit of a breather after the main course. If you think you need more time, serve the cheese platter while you get the pudding in the oven.

There follow some suggested meals using the recipes in the book which will suit all sorts of occasions – they probably break some, if not all, of the rules given above, but might at least give you ideas to get you started.

Seafood special

Creole potted prawns
(page 31)

or Individual smoked salmon pots
(page 32)

Italian cod and garlic tomatoes
(page 56)

Baked nectarines and cherries
(page 125)

Summer Sunday roast

Roast asparagus and poached egg
(page 26)

or Summer minestrone soup
(page 12)

Roast sea bass with Romesco sauce
(page 58)

Baked Alaska
(page 122)

Elegant evening

Prawn bisque
(page 18)

Venison with herbed pumpkin wedges
(page 101)

Golden mash
(page 111)

Green beans with crispy Parma ham
(page 106)

Melting chocolate puddings
(page 130)

Asian banquet

Thai prawn salad
(page 31)

Chinese tangerine beef casserole
(page 85) served with boiled rice and
stir-fried Chinese greens

Mango and coconut terrine
(page 132)

Italian job

Aubergine and mozzarella stacks
(page 28)

or Roasted red pepper soup
(page 13)

Pan-fried beef with garlic, rosemary
and balsamic vinegar (page 86)

Panna cotta with Cointreau sauce
(page 134)

Mediterranean barbecue

Baba ghanoush
(page 26)

or Mushrooms and artichokes à la Grecque
(page 24)

Moroccan lamb burgers
(page 90)

Summer fruits jelly
(page 135

Oriental-style Sunday lunch

Shredded chicken noodle soup
(page 20)

Oriental lamb with mushrooms
(page 92)

Coconut soufflé with spiced pineapple
(page 124)

French feast

Garlicky mushroom toasts
(page 24)

or Pork and duck rillettes
(page 35)

Pan-fried salmon with Pernod sauce
(page 64)

Cointreau crêpes
(page 123)

Indian-style Sunday lunch

Cream of pumpkin soup
(page 14)

Spiced honey-roasted poussins
(page 72)

Roasted roots with Indian spices
(page 105)

Plum and banana crumbles
(page 121)

Teenager's birthday party

Smoked haddock chowder
(page 19)

Caribbean barbecued jerk ribs
(page 98)

Potato and pastrami salad
(page 117)

Tiramisu gâteau
(page 137)

Buffet party for 8–10

Pork and duck rillettes
(page 35)

Chicken and bean salad with crisp chorizo
(page 79) served with buttered new potatoes

Mango and coconut terrine
(page 132)

Grand picnic

Mexican beef tortillas
(page 48)

Salmon and watercress puff
(page 65)

Potato and pastrami salad
(page 117)

Goats' cheese, pear and blackberry tart
(page 127)

Index

Picture credits

BBC Worldwide would like to thank the following for providing photographs and permission to reproduce copyright material. While every effort has been made to trace and acknowledge all copyright holders, we would like to apologize should there have been any errors or omissions.

Abbreviations: l left, r right
Photographs © BBC Worldwide/Jean Cazals: pages 2, 5l & r, 6, 10–21, 36l & r, 37r, 39, 44–45, 49, 50l, 51l & r, 53–59, 61–67, 68r, 72–76, 79–80, 82l & r, 83r, 86–89, 92–93, 97, 100–101, 102, 103l & r, 105–136. © BBC Worldwide/Phillip Webb: pages 4, 21, 22–35, 37l, 40–43,

46, 50r, 52, 69l, 70–71, 81, 83l, 84–85, 94–96, 104. © BBC Worldwide/Marie-Louise Avery: pages 38, 48, 60, 77, 78, 90, 98. © BBC Worldwide/Sìan Irvine: page 68l. © BBC Worldwide/Nicola Browne: page 22l.